Introduction

Crochet as we know it is just the tip of the iceberg. Over time, the craft has taken a specific path, resulting in the familiar, easily recognizable styles we see today. But crochet has so much more to offer – a world of endless possibilities waiting to be explored.

In recent years, new stitches, techniques, aesthetics, and styles have emerged, reshaping the boundaries of traditional crochet. I'm thrilled to be part of this evolution, sharing fresh ideas and demonstrating how even the simplest crochet stitches can become something extraordinary.

Crochet offers an incredible sense of freedom. At its core, almost every crochet stitch is made up of six yarn strands – four forming its leg and two creating the top loop. This unique structure provides various options for where to work the next stitch. These options, combined with the choice of stitches to make and how to make them, create limitless possibilities for designing new patterns and textures.

As a crochet designer, I am deeply inspired by these myriad possibilities. I love to invent new stitches, experiment with unconventional techniques, and create designs that showcase unique textures and fresh, modern aesthetics. Through this book, I hope to inspire you to explore new horizons in crochet and view it in an entirely new light.

Let's uncover the hidden potential of crochet, one stitch at a time!

NEW WAYS WITH CROCHET

50 innovative crochet stitch patterns and projects

Olena Fedotova

DAVID & CHARLES
— PUBLISHING —

www.davidandcharles.com

Contents

Tools and materials

Yarn

The stitch pattern swatches in this book were created using Malabrigo Rios yarn (100% superwash Merino wool, aran/worsted weight, 100g skein, 192m/210yds) and a 5mm (US size H/8) hook.

Each chapter is highlighted with carefully chosen shades of Malabrigo Rios to reflect its theme and mood:

Chapter 1: Pearl (RIO036), a soft light grey, evokes the refined textures of sand and stone, complementing the chapter's focus on simple and elegant stitches.

Chapter 2: Apple Green (RIO011) and Ankara Green (RIO413) paired with Natural (RIO063) bring energy and vibrancy, reflecting botanical elements like fresh grass and flower fields.

Chapter 3: Cian (RIO683), a vivid blue, symbolizes flowing water, wave-like textures, and the boundless expanse of the sky.

Chapter 4: Frank Ochre (RIO035), a rich golden hue, captures the earthy tones of roots, vines, and bark, mirroring the deep forest theme.

Chapter 5: Hollyhock (RIO148), a lush purple, highlights intricate crochet cables, offering a bold and striking conclusion to the book.

While Malabrigo Rios was chosen for its excellent stitch definition, texture, and versatility, these stitch patterns can be worked with any yarn weight or fiber of your choice. Simply adjust the hook size to suit your selected yarn to ensure smooth stitching and the achievement of the desired drape and proportions.

Hooks

Crochet hooks come in a variety of materials, shapes, and sizes, each offering a different feel and experience. Aluminum hooks are smooth and lightweight, while wooden and bamboo hooks provide warmth and a bit more friction. Ergonomic hooks with soft or contoured handles can help reduce hand strain. I prefer lightweight metal hooks with a smooth finish and no handle. A sharper tip is essential for me – it makes it easier to work through stitches smoothly.

Notions

STITCH MARKERS

Stitch markers are extremely useful tools for marking a specific stitch or point in your pattern. Crochet stitch markers come in a variety of forms, including spiral hooks, plastic safety pins and locking hooks. Choose something light and easy to see!

YARN NEEDLE

A blunt-tipped needle is essential for weaving in ends. Choose one with a large enough eye for your yarn weight.

TAPE MEASURE

Make sure you have a tape measure handy at all times for measuring your tension (gauge) or projects as you go. Choose one that is not likely to stretch or warp.

SHARP SCISSORS

A pair of small, sharp embroidery scissors or yarn snips is a must.

BLOCKING MAT AND PINS

You can buy special blocking mats and pins for knitted and crocheted pieces. Alternatively, lay your damp pieces out on a towel or absorbent surface and pin in place. Soft jigsaw tiles are also popular, as you can make your blocking surface the size you need and then pack it away again easily.

About this book

This book takes you on a creative adventure through the world of crochet, providing inspiration and instructions to help you discover new stitches, patterns, and textures. Its five chapters highlight specific stitches and techniques, each showcasing a fresh perspective on crochet's creative potential.

Chapter 1 focuses on foundational stitches and textures. These patterns feature simple crochet stitches used in innovative ways to create refined and versatile fabrics. Don't forget to check the wrong side of your swatches – almost all the stitch patterns in Chapter 1 have equally beautiful and interesting textures on both sides.

Chapter 2 introduces colorful, dynamic designs and a new stitch: the raised double crochet. This stitch allows you to create textured lines over the linen stitch pattern, producing a variety of effects from gentle textures to bold lines and striking colorwork.

Chapter 3 takes you into the world of flowing water, featuring stitch patterns that mimic wave-like textures and fluid designs. These patterns are created by pairing textured ridge lines, formed with single-crochet ribbing worked in the back loops, with a variety of other stitches such as eyelets, circles, and diamond motifs. This chapter also introduces an innovative technique that allows you to outline these shapes with ridge lines, maintaining their continuous flow.

Chapter 4 delves into deep, organic textures inspired by forest roots, vines, and bark. This chapter introduces a unique combination of the extended single crochet stitch worked over the linen stitch pattern, creating entirely new crochet surfaces.

Chapter 5 concludes the journey with bold and striking crochet cables, worked in a truly unique way. In a break with traditional methods, these cables are created horizontally, adding one wave at a time to form stunning, flowing designs.

Each chapter begins with an explanation of its main stitch or technique, accompanied by photographs to make the patterns approachable and easy to follow for all skill levels. Every stitch pattern includes detailed instructions and clear charts (where applicable) to support visual learners. Chapters 1 and 5, which focus on unusual ways of working stitches, provide step-by-step photographs instead of charts to give a clearer visual idea.

Additionally, I encourage you to rotate the book to see how the stitch patterns look when worked top down or diagonally – sometimes a change in direction transforms the design completely.

The projects in this book have been made using metric measurements, and the imperial equivalents provided have been calculated following standard conversion practices. The imperial measurements are rounded to the nearest ¼in for ease of use; however, if you need more exact measurements, there are a number of excellent online converters that you can use. Always use either metric or imperial measurements, not a combination of both.

Whether you're looking to expand your crochet skills or simply find inspiration for your next project, this book is here to guide you. Dive into the chapters, explore the stitches, and enjoy discovering new possibilities in crochet!

STITCHES AND TECHNIQUES

All the patterns in this book use US crochet terminology. UK equivalents are provided in the abbreviations table, which you will find in General Techniques: Basic Stitches.

The stitch patterns in this book are versatile, and designed to be used in a variety of projects. Each pattern is worked over a minimum number of stitches, which is given at the start of each pattern. Pattern repeats are worked over multiples of this number. For example, a 12-stitch pattern can be worked over 24 stitches, 36 stitches, 48 stitches, and so on.

Standard stitch information can be found in General Techniques: Basic Stitches.

Special stitches that are the foundation of a chapter are detailed in the chapter introduction as follows:

Chapter 1 Extended single crochet

Chapter 2 Raised double crochet

Chapter 3 Twisted single crochet

Chapter 4 Extended single crochet two rows below

Chapter 5 Foundation single crochet

Instructions for all other special stitches can be found in General Techniques: Special Stitches.

HOW TO USE THE CHARTS IN THIS BOOK

The charts in this book provide a visual representation of the written instructions. They can be particularly useful if you need clarification of part of the written pattern, and can be used instead of the written instructions. The charts for each stitch pattern show at least two stitch and row repeats. On single-color stitch patterns, stitches are highlighted when they are worked in an unusual way or need particular attention.

For example, on the chart shown here, the end sc worked on Row 6 is in red, to differentiate it from the sc BLO stitches worked on the rest of the row. On two-color charts, each color yarn is represented by a different color stitch, and stitches that need attention are represented in blue. The charts for the projects have their own specific instructions so that you can follow them without referring to the written pattern if you wish.

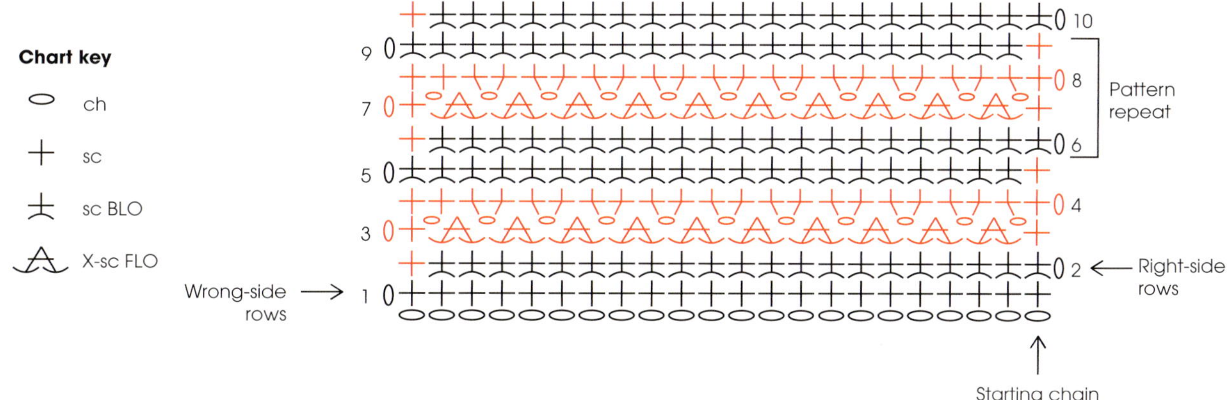

CHAPTER 1:
SIMPLE STITCHES

Even basic, well-known stitches can surprise us with new textures and details when viewed from a fresh angle. This chapter explores these hidden possibilities, showing what happens when familiar stitches are worked in an unusual way, adjusted slightly, or combined with others in creative combinations.

This chapter draws inspiration from the grounding elements of nature - stone, soil, sand - surfaces that reveal a quiet beauty in their simplicity. It uses the smallest crochet stitches to create textures that capture the essence of these earthy details.

STITCH FOCUS:

Extended single crochet

NOTES ON TECHNIQUE

One of the most common stitches in this chapter, and throughout the book, is the extended single crochet (esc). When completed, it forms two stacked Vs, with top loops that look the same as those of any other crochet stitch. The esc is softer and stretchier than a regular single crochet, with a height close to that of a double crochet.

SPECIAL STITCHES

Extended single crochet (esc): insert hook into indicated st or sp, yo, pull up a loop (A), yo, draw through 1 loop on hook (B), yo, draw through both loops on hook to complete the st.

A

The hook with one loop pulled through the space it is worked into.

B

Two loops on hook, after drawing through the first loop on hook.

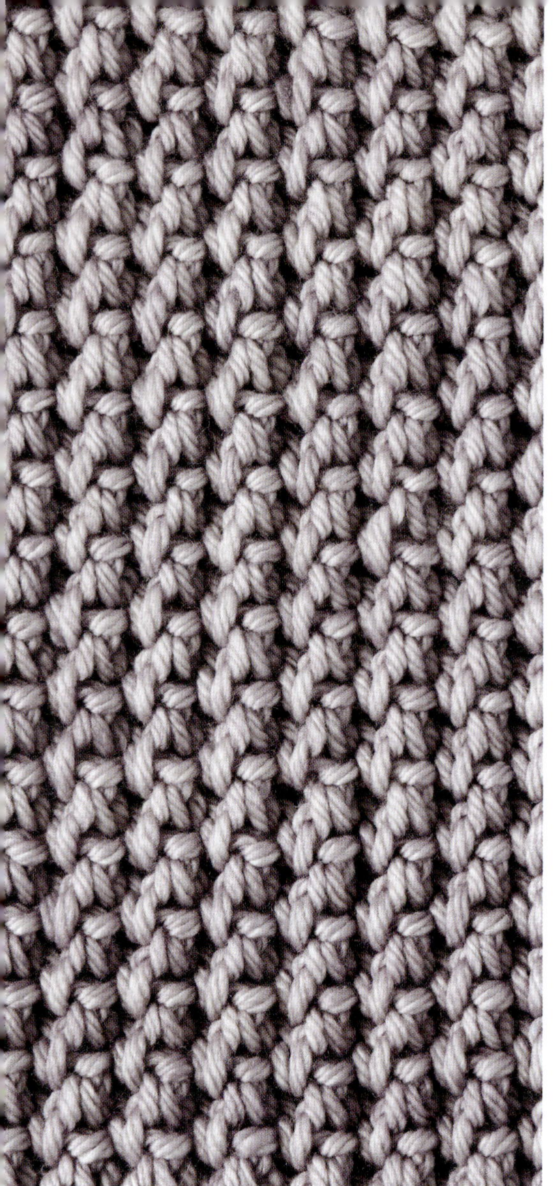

COBBLESTONE STITCH

Creates a warm, textured, squishy fabric that is equally interesting on the reverse side. Perfect for projects where versatility and texture are key.

Note: *this pattern is worked over a multiple of 2 sts. Starting chains do not count as sts throughout.*

Start: Chain a multiple of 2 sts plus 1.

Row 1 (RS): 1 sc in back ridge (bump) of second ch from hook, 1 sc in back ridge (bump) of each ch to end. Turn.

Row 2 (WS): Ch 1, 2 sc, *ch 1, sk 1 st, 1 sc; rep from * to end. Turn.

Row 3: Ch 1, 1 sc, *sc2tog in next ch-sp and first leg of next sc†, ch 1; rep from * to last st, 1 sc. Turn.

Row 4: Ch 1, 1 sc, *1 sc in next ch-sp, ch 1; rep from *to last st, 1 sc. Turn.

Rep Rows 3 and 4 for pattern.

†How to: Insert hook in ch-sp, yo, pull up a loop (2 loops on hook), insert hook through the first leg of next sc in direction of work (A), yo, pull up a loop (3 loops on hook), yo, draw through all 3 loops on hook.

Back

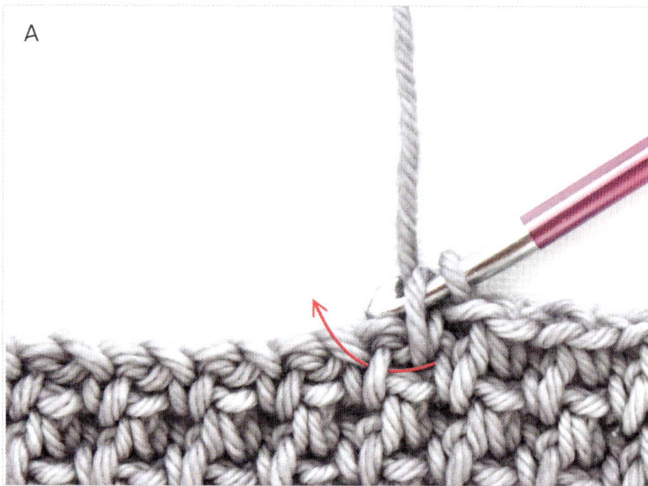

Insert the hook into the first leg of the next sc in the direction of the work (direction of the arrow).

SANDPIPER STITCH

Delicate eyelets create a unique and beautiful texture, with a distinct pattern on each side.

Note: *this pattern is worked over a multiple of 2 sts. Starting chains do not count as sts throughout.*

Start: Chain a multiple of 2 plus 1.

Row 1 (RS): 1 sc in back ridge (bump) of second ch from hook, 1 sc in back ridge (bump) of each ch to end. Turn.

Row 2 (WS): Ch 1, 2 sc, *ch 1, sk 1 st, 1 sc; rep from * to end. Turn.

Row 3: Ch 1, 1 sc, ch 1, sc2tog in next 2 ch-sps, ch 1, *sc2tog in ch-sp just worked and next ch-sp, ch 1; rep from * to last ch-sp, sc2tog in last ch-sp and next st, 1 sc. Turn.

Row 4: Ch 1, 1 esc, *ch 1, 1 esc in ch-sp (B); rep from * to last st, 1 esc. Turn.

Row 5: Ch 1, 1 sc, sc2tog in next st and ch-sp, ch 1, *sc2tog in ch-sp just worked and next ch-sp, ch 1; rep from * to last st, 1 sc. Turn.

Row 6: Ch 1, 1 esc, *1 esc in ch-sp, ch 1; rep from * to last 2 sts, sk 1 st, 1 esc. Turn.

Rep Rows 3–6 for pattern.

Back

Arrow indicates the stitch under which to work the esc (into the ch-sp or st beneath).

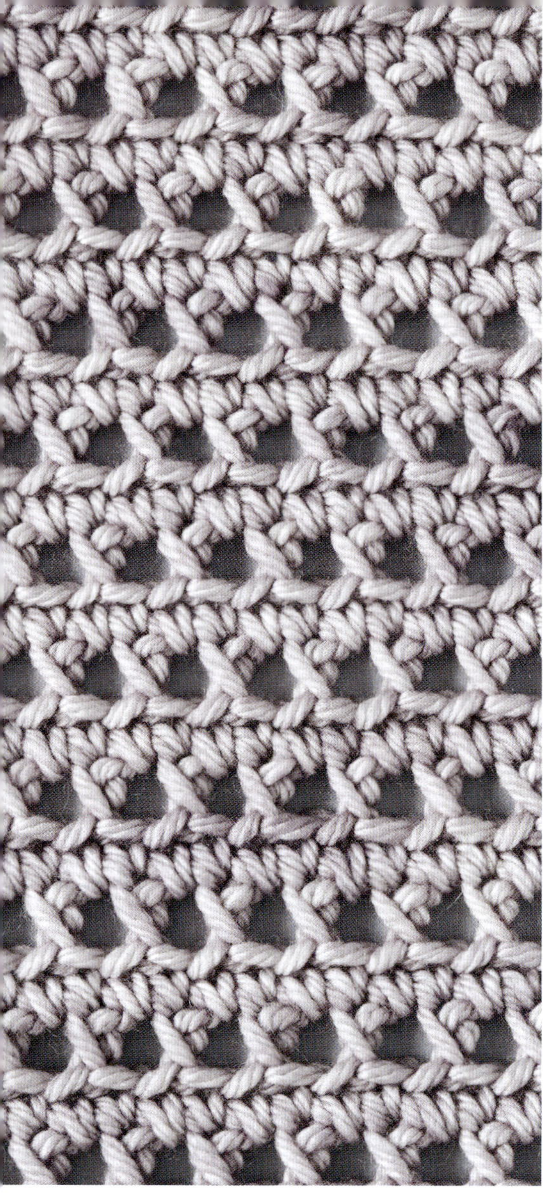

TWISTED EYELET STITCH

Creates a lacy, airy fabric with eyelets, perfect for lightweight, breezy projects.

Note: *this pattern is worked over a multiple of 2 sts. Starting chains do not count as sts throughout.*

Start: Chain a multiple of 2 plus 1.

Row 1 (RS): 1 sc in back ridge (bump) of second ch from hook, 1 sc in back ridge (bump) of each ch to end. Turn.

Row 2: Ch 1, esc in back loops of 2 sts at the same time†, *ch 1, esc in back loops of 2 sts at the same time; rep from * to end, hdc in both loops of st just worked. Turn.

Row 3: Ch 1, 1 sc in each st and ch-sp to end. Turn.

Row 4: Ch 1, 1 esc in both loops of first st, *esc in back loops of 2 sts at the same time, ch 1; rep from * to last st, 1 hdc. Turn.

Row 5: Rep Row 3.

Rep Rows 2–5 for pattern.

†How to: Insert your hook in back loop of first st from front to back, then insert it in back loop of second st from back to front (A), yo and pull up a loop, yo, draw through 1 loop on hook, yo, draw through both loops on hook.

Back

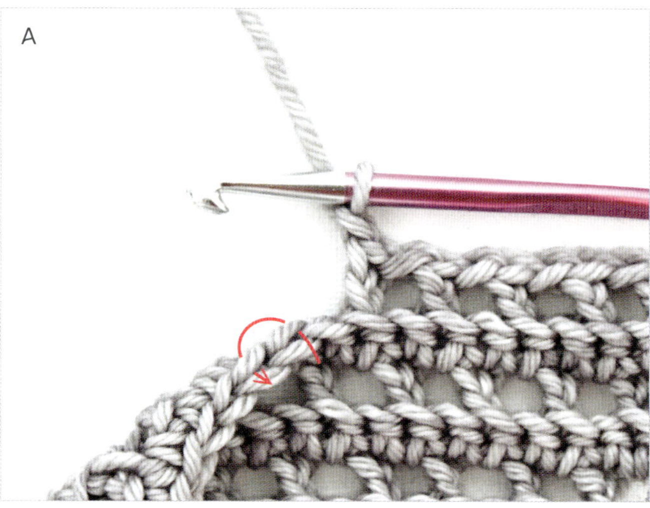

Insert the hook into the back loop of the first st from front to back, and then into the back loop of second st from back to front.

ROPE RIDGE STITCH

Creates a thick, elastic fabric with bold horizontal ribbing, which adds both texture and stretch. For drape and airiness use fine yarn with a larger hook, and work the stitches more loosely.

Note: *this pattern can be worked over any number of sts. Starting chains do not count as sts throughout.*

Start: Chain any number of sts plus 1.

Row 1 (RS): 1 sc in back ridge (bump) of second ch from hook, 1 sc in back ridge (bump) of each ch to end. Turn.

Row 2: Ch 1, sc2tog BLO†, *sc2tog BLO in last st worked and next st; rep from * to end, 1 sc in both loops of last st worked. Turn.

Row 3: Ch 1, 1 sc FLO in each st to last st, 1 sc in both loops of last st. Turn.

Rep Rows 2 and 3 for pattern.

†How to: Insert your hook in back loop of first st, then insert it in back loop of next st (B), yo and pull up a loop, yo, draw through both loops on hook.

Back

Insert the hook into the back loop of the first st, and then into the back loop of the second st.

DOUBLE DASH STITCH

Creates a solid, structured fabric; the short horizontal lines and subtle ribbed effect give it a beautiful texture.

Note: *this pattern can be worked over any number of sts. Starting chains do not count as sts throughout.*

Start: Chain any number of sts plus 1.

Row 1 (RS): 1 sc in back ridge (bump) of second ch from hook, 1 sc in back ridge (bump) of each ch to end. Turn.

Row 2: Ch 1, esc2tog BLO, *1 esc in BLO of last st worked and next st at the same time (A); rep from * to end, 1 hdc in last st. Turn.

Row 3: Ch 1, 1 sc in each st to end. Turn.

Row 4: Ch 1, 1 esc BLO in first st, *esc2tog BLO in st just worked and next st; rep from * to last st, (1 esc in BLO of last st worked, 1 sc in both loops of last st at the same time)†.

Row 5: Rep Row 3.

Rep Rows 2–5 for pattern.

†How to: Insert your hook in last 2 back loops, yo and pull up a loop, yo, draw through 1 loop on hook (partial esc), insert hook in both loops of last st, yo and pull up a loop (3 loops on hook), yo, draw through 3 loops on hook.

Back

Working in BLO, insert the hook from front to back into the st just worked and from back to front into the next st.

V-RIDGE STITCH

Creates a very squishy, stretchy ribbing with defined horizontal rows of V-shaped stitches. The reverse offers a different but equally interesting ribbed texture, making this ideal for reversible projects.

Note: *this pattern can be worked over any number of sts. Starting chains do not count as sts throughout.*

Start: Chain any number of sts plus 1.

Row 1 (RS): Ch 1 (does not count as a st), 1 sc in back ridge (bump) of each ch. Turn.

Row 2: Ch 1, 1 sc, *1 Rib st beg in second leg of st just worked and continuing in BLO of next st (B); rep from * to last st, 1 Rib st in both loops of last st. Turn.

Row 3: Ch 1, 1 sc BLO in each st to last st, 1 sc. Turn.

Note: *after Row 3, you will see that the first leg and front loops of the scs from Row 2 sit on the RS of the work, creating what looks like a chain.*

Rep Rows 2 and 3 for pattern.

Back

Insert the hook into the second leg of sc or rib st just made.

RIPPLE TEXTURE STITCH

Creates a sleek, smooth, and surprisingly fine lightweight fabric, even when worked with thicker yarns.

Note: *this pattern can be worked over any number of sts. Starting chains do not count as sts throughout.*

Start: Chain any number of sts plus 1.

Row 1 (WS): 1 sc in back ridge (bump) of second ch from hook, 1 sc in back ridge (bump) of each ch to end. Turn.

Row 2 (RS): Ch 1, starting in first st *yo from front to back, insert hook in next st from front to back (A), yo, pull up a loop, draw through first loop on hook, yo, draw through 2 loops on hook; rep from * to end. Turn.

Row 3: Ch 1, starting in first st *yo from back to front, insert hook in next st from back to front, yo, pull up a loop, draw through first loop on hook, yo, draw through 2 loops on hook; rep from * to last st, 1 sc. Turn.

Rep Rows 2 and 3 for pattern.

Back

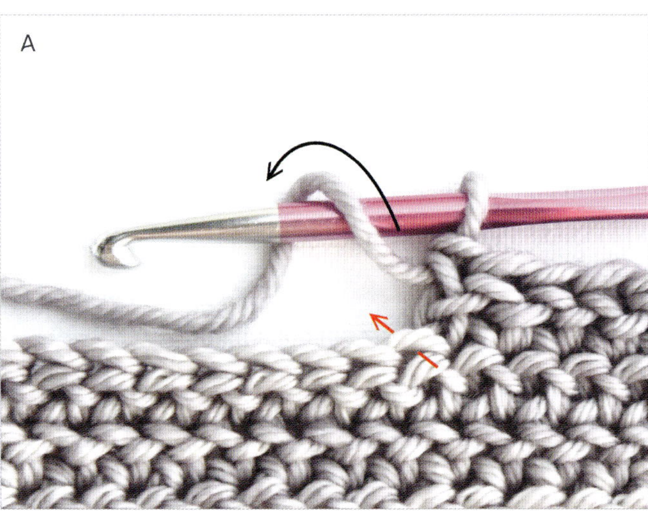

Take the yarn over the hook from front to back (black arrow) and insert hook into the st from front to back (red arrow).

TWIN LEAF STITCH

Creates a light, open fabric with plenty of airflow. The clustered stitches give it structure, while the open spaces create drape, making it ideal for breathable projects.

Note: *this pattern is worked over a multiple of 3 sts plus 2.*

Start: Chain a multiple of 3 plus 2.

Row 1 (WS): 1 sc in second ch from hook, *ch 2, sk 2 chs, 1 sc; rep from * to last ch, 1 sc in last ch. Turn.

Row 2 (RS): Ch 2 (counts as 1 dc), 1 Beg Lst, *ch 2, 1 Lst in st just worked, next ch-sp and next st; rep from * to end, 1 dc in last st (just worked). Turn.

Row 3: Rep Row 2, inserting hook into sts and ch-sps from back to front (B) when working Beg Lst and Lst. Turn.

Rep Rows 2 and 3 for pattern.

Back

On WS rows, insert hook into ch-sp from back to front.

MARIGOLD STITCH

Creates a beautiful floral texture, perfect for adding depth and dimension to your projects. It works wonderfully with both solid and variegated yarns, and its versatility suits it to a variety of designs.

Note: *this pattern is worked over a multiple of 4 sts. Starting chains do not count as sts throughout.*

Start: Chain a multiple of 4 plus 1.

Row 1 (RS): 1 sc in back ridge (bump) of second ch from hook, 1 sc in back ridge (bump) of each ch to end. Turn.

Row 2: Ch 1, 1 sc BLO, *3-spike Star-st, 2 sc BLO; rep from * to last 3 sts, 3-spike Star-st, 1 sc. Turn.

Row 3: Ch 1, 1 sc BLO, *2 hdc in top of Star-st, 2 sc BLO; rep from * to last Star-st, 2 hdc in top of last Star-st, 1 sc. Turn.

Row 4: Ch 1, 3 sc BLO, *3-spike Star-st, 6 sc BLO; rep from * to last 3 sts, 2 sc BLO, 1 sc. Turn.

Row 5: Ch 1, 3 sc BLO, *2 hdc in top of Star-st (A, red arrows), 2 sc BLO (A, black arrows); rep from * to last Star-st, 2 hdc in top of last Star-st, 2 sc BLO, 1 sc. Turn.

Rep Rows 2–5 for pattern.

Back

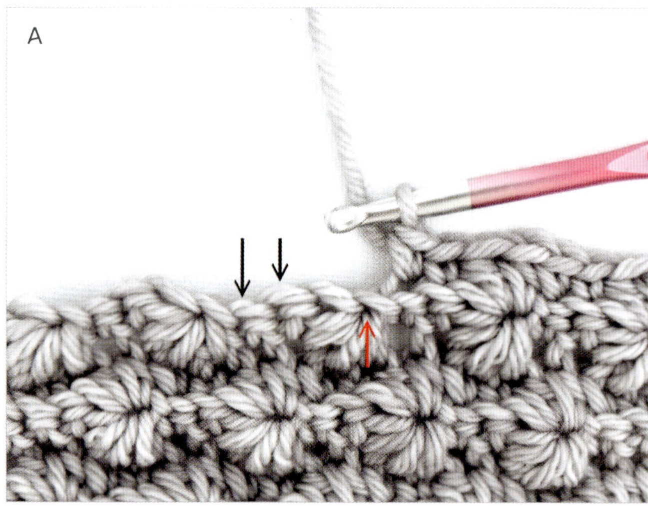

The red arrow indicates where to work the 2 hdc. The black arrows indicate the 2 sts into which the 2 sc BLO are worked. The ch between them remains unworked.

EVENING STAR STITCH

Creates a softly textured pattern of small elongated starbursts.

Note: *this pattern is worked over a multiple of 2 sts. Starting chains do not count as sts throughout.*

Start: Chain a multiple of 2 plus 1.

Row 1 (RS): 1 sc in second ch from hook, *ch 1, sk 1 ch, 1 sc; rep from * to end. Turn.

Row 2 (WS): Ch 1, *1 Y-st†, ch 1; rep from * to last st, 1 esc. Turn.

Row 3: Ch 1, 1 sc, sc2tog into Y st and ch-sp‡, *ch 1, sc2tog into Y st and ch-sp; rep from * to end, 1 esc in both loops of last ch-sp worked. Turn.

Row 4: Ch 1, 1 sc, *1 Y-st, ch 1; rep from * to last 2 sts, 1 Y-st in BLO of next st and both loops of last st, 1 hdc in last st. Turn.

Row 5: Ch 1, 1 sc, ch 1, sk 1 Y-st, *sc2tog into Y st and ch-sp, ch 1; rep from * to last st, 1 esc.

Rep Rows 2–5 for pattern.

†Y-st: Yo, insert hook in BLO of st from back to front, yo, pull up a loop, insert hook under next ch-sp from back to front, yo, pull up a loop (4 loops on hook), yo, draw through all 4 loops on hook.

‡Sc2tog into Y st and ch-sp: Insert hook in top of Y-st (B, red arrow), yo, pull up a loop, insert hook into BLO of next ch (B, black arrow), yo, pull up a loop, yo, draw though all 3 loops on hook.

Back

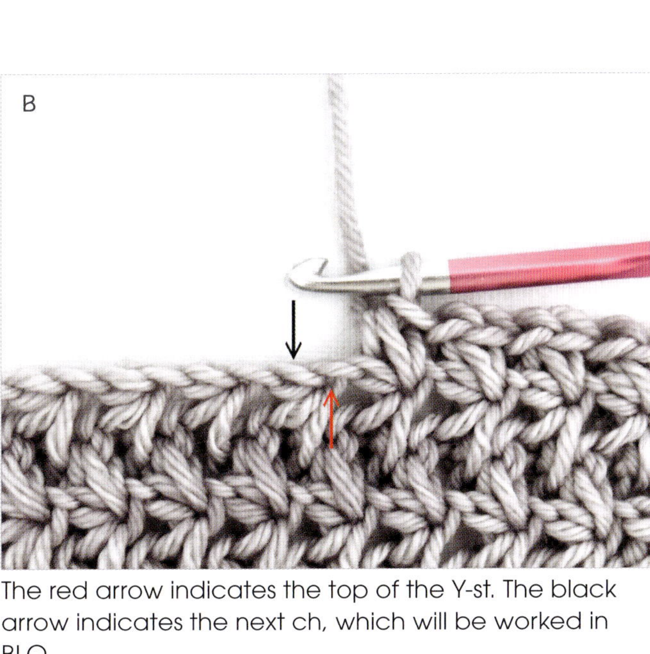

The red arrow indicates the top of the Y-st. The black arrow indicates the next ch, which will be worked in BLO.

SIMPLE STITCHES PROJECT

Daydream Shawl

Daydream is an asymmetrical shawl worked in two stages. A wide leaf stitch panel is created first, worked from corner to corner. Once complete, the body of the shawl is worked along one edge of the panel, gradually decreasing to a point.

The Daydream shawl features a variety of stitch patterns that take you on a quiet, thoughtful journey of stitch exploration.

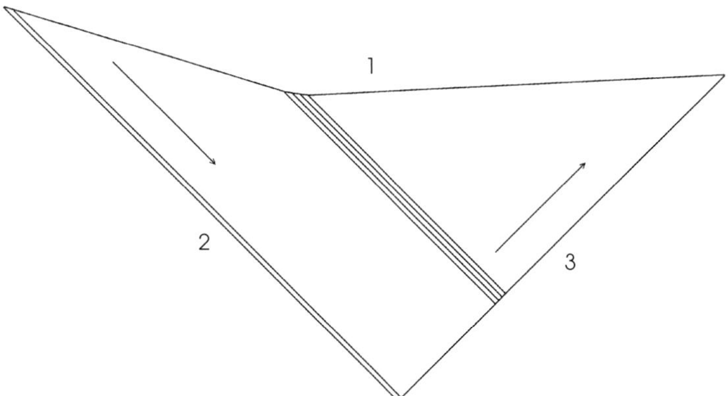

YOU WILL NEED

YARN

Malabrigo Sock (100% Merino wool), 3-ply/lightfingering, 100g (402m/440yds), in the following shade: Alice (SW340); 2 skeins

HOOKS

Size 3.5mm (US E/4) hook
Size 3.75mm (US F/5) hook

TENSION

26 sts (sc and chs) and 22 rows measure 10 x 10cm (4 x 4in) over Linen st using a 3.75mm (US F/5) hook.

9 Lsts and 11 rows measure 10 x 10cm (4 x 4in) over Leaf st using a 3.5mm hook.

MEASUREMENTS

Wingspan (1): 147cm (58in), including 60cm (23½in) along the insert and 87cm (34¼in) along the body

Left edge (2): 114cm (45in)

Right edge (3): 96cm (37¾in)

ABBREVIATIONS

beg	beginning
BLO	back loop only
ch	chain
ch-sp	chain space
dc	double crochet
hdc	half double crochet
htr	half treble crochet
rep	repeat
RS	right side of work
sc	single crochet
sc2tog	single crochet 2 sts together
sk	skip/miss
sp	space
st(s)	stitch(es)
WS	wrong side of work

SPECIAL STITCHES

Extended single crochet (esc) (see Chapter 1: Special Stitches)

Beginning Leaf st (Beg Lst) (see General Techniques: Special Stitches)

Leaf st (Lst) (see General Techniques: Special Stitches)

Rib stitch (Rib st) (see Chapter 1: V-Ridge Stitch and General Techniques: Special Stitches)

INSTRUCTIONS

LEFT PANEL

Note: *when working Leaf st on the WS rows, remember to work from back to front (see General Techniques: Special Stitches).*

Row 1 (WS): Using smaller hook, ch 5, 1 hdc in fifth ch from hook. Turn. (1 dc, 1 hdc, 1 ch-sp)

Row 2 (RS): Ch 3 (counts as 1 dc throughout), Beg Lst in ch2-sp and third ch of beg 5ch from Row 1, ch 2, 1 htr in same (third) ch. Turn. (3 sts, 1 ch-sp)

Row 3: Ch 5 (counts as 1 dc and 1 ch-sp throughout), 1 Lst in htr, ch-sp and top of beg Lst, ch 1, 1 dc in top of beg 3ch from last row. Turn. (2 dc, 1 Lst, 2 ch-sp)

Row 4: Ch 3, 1 Beg Lst in ch-sp and next st, ch 2, 1 Lst in same st, ch2-sp and third ch of beg 5ch from Row 3, ch 2, 1 htr in same (third) ch. Turn. (1 dc, 2 Lst, 1 htr, 2 ch-sp)

Row 5: Ch 5, 1 Lst in htr, ch2-sp and next st, ch 2, 1 Lst in same st, next ch2-sp and next st, ch 1, 1 dc in top of beg 3ch from last row. Turn. (2 dc, 2 Lst, 3 ch-sp)

Row 6: Ch 3, 1 Beg Lst in ch-sp and next st, ch 2, 1 Lst in same st, next ch2-sp and next st, ch 2, 1 Lst st just worked, ch2-sp and third ch of beg 5ch from last row ch 2, 1 htr in same (third) ch. Turn. (1 dc, 3 Lst, 1 htr, 3 ch-sp)

Row 7: Ch 5, 1 Lst in htr, ch2-sp and next st), *ch 2, 1 Lst in same st, next ch2-sp and next st; rep from * once more, ch 1, 1 dc in top of beg 3ch from last row. Turn. (2 dc, 3 Lst, 4 ch-sp)

Row 8: Ch 3, 1 Beg Lst in ch-sp and next st, *ch 2, 1 Lst in same st, next ch-sp and next st; rep from * to last ch2-sp, ch 2, 1 Lst in same st, ch2-sp and third ch of beg 5ch from Row 7, ch 2, 1 htr in same (third) ch. Turn. (1 Lst increased)

Row 9: Ch 5, 1 Lst in htr, ch2-sp and next st, *ch 2, 1 Lst in st just worked, next ch2-sp and next st; rep from * to last st, ch 1, 1 dc in top of beg 3ch from last row. Turn. (1 ch-sp increased)

Rows 10–49: Rep Rows 8 and 9 another 20 times. (2 dc, 24 Lst, 25 ch-sp)

Row 50: Ch 3, 1 Beg Lst in ch-sp and next st, *ch 2, 1 Lst in same st, next ch-sp and next st; rep from * to last ch2-sp, ch 2, 1 Lst in same st, ch2-sp and third ch of beg 5ch, ch 1, 1 htr in same (third) ch. Turn. (25 Lst, 25 ch-sp)

Row 51: Ch 3, 1 Beg Lst in first ch-sp and next st, *ch 2, 1 Lst in st just worked, next ch2-sp and next st); rep from * to last st, ch 1, 1 dc in top of beg 3ch from last row. Turn.

Rows 52–120: Rep Row 51 another 69 times.

Do not turn. Do not cut yarn. Proceed to Right Triangle.

I suggest blocking your work at this stage. Consider slightly stretching it widthways rather than lengthways during blocking.

RIGHT TRIANGLE

Rotate the piece so that you are ready to work along the row ends.

Note: *starting ch 1 does not count as a st throughout.*

Row 1 (RS): Ch 1, (2 sc in next ch3-sp, 2 sc in side of next dc) 34 times, 2 sc in next ch3-sp, 1 sc in side of next dc, sc2tog in side of dc just worked and next ch3-sp. Turn. (140 sts)

Row 2: Ch 1, sk 1 st, 1 sc, work Rib st to last st, 1 Rib st in both loops of last st. Turn. (1 st decreased)

Row 3: Ch 1, 1 sc BLO in each st to last 3 sts, sc2tog BLO, 1 sc. Turn. (1 st decreased)

Row 4: Ch 1, sk 1 st, 1 sc, esc in back loops of 2 sts at the same time, *ch 1, esc in back loops of 2 sts at the same time; rep from * to end, 1 sc in last st (just worked). Turn. (2 sc, 68 esc, 67 ch-sp)

Row 5: Ch 1, 1 sc in each st and ch-sp to last ch-sp, sc2tog in last ch-sp and next esc, 1 sc. Turn. (136 sts)

Row 6: Rep Row 2. (135 sts)

Row 7: Rep Row 3. (134 sts)

Change to larger hook.

Row 8: Ch 1, sk 1 st, 1 sc, *ch 1, sk 1 st, 1 sc; rep from * to end. Turn. (67 sc, 66 ch)

Row 9: Ch 1, 1 sc, 1 sc in next ch-sp, *ch 1, 1 sc in next ch-sp; rep from * to last ch-sp, ch 1, sc2tog in last ch-sp and last st. Turn. (67 sc, 65 ch)

Row 10: Ch 1, *1 sc in next ch-sp, ch 1; rep from * to last 2 sts, sk 1 st, 1 sc. Turn. (1 sc decreased)

Row 11: Ch 1, 1 sc, 1 sc in next ch-sp, *ch 1, 1 sc in next ch-sp; rep from * to last ch-sp, ch 1, sc2tog in last ch-sp and last st. Turn. (1 ch-sp decreased)

Rows 10 and 11 form Linen St pattern.

Rep Rows 10 and 11, decreasing as set, until 3 sc and 1 ch-sp remain, ending after a WS row.

Next Row (RS): Ch 1, sk 1 st, 1 sc in next ch-sp, ch 1, sk 1 st, 1 sc. Turn. (2 sc, 1 ch-sp)

Next Row: Ch 1, 1 sc, sc2tog in next ch-sp and last st. Turn. (2 sc)

Last Row: Ch 1, sk 1 st, 1 sc. (1 sc)

Cut yarn and fasten off.

EDGING

Change to smaller hook.

With RS facing, join yarn in first ch of Left Panel and prepare to work across row ends along the long edge of the panel.

Row 1 (RS): Ch 1, 1 sc in ch, *2 sc in next ch3-sp, 2 sc in side of next dc; rep from * to end of long side. Turn. (241 sts)

Row 2: Ch 1, 1 sc BLO, work Rib st to end, 1 Rib st in both loops of last st (just worked). Turn. (242 sts)

Row 3: Ch 1, 2 sc BLO in first st, 1 sc BLO in each st to last st, 1 sc. Turn. (243 sts)

Fasten off and weave in ends.

FINISHING

Wet block your shawl to the finished measurements. Lay the wet shawl out on a flat surface. Align the edges to given dimensions (note that the wingspan is not a straight line). Pin in place and let it dry completely.

CHAPTER 2:

LINEN STITCH VARIATIONS

In this chapter, the well-known linen stitch pattern is used as a base, and some of the single crochet stitches are replaced with raised double crochet stitches. This creates various effects, ranging from subtle textures to bold lines and striking colorwork.

STITCH FOCUS:

Raised double crochet

NOTES ON TECHNIQUE

Raised double crochet stitches (rdc) are always worked on RS rows into stitches two rows below the chain space. Work them into the two front strands of the leg of the indicated stitch: either single crochet (A) or raised double crochet (B).

The raised effect is similar to that created by front post stitches; the difference is that the textured line created with rdc looks like a vertical row of loops or chains.

The ch-sp above the stitch you have just worked should be skipped, as if you had worked into it on a regular linen stitch pattern. For example, if the pattern says: (rdc, ch 1, 1 sc), work it as follows: rdc into the stitch below the ch-sp, leave the ch-sp itself unworked, ch 1, 1 sc in the next ch-sp.

SPECIAL STITCHES

Raised double crochet (rdc): yo, insert hook under 2 front strands of leg of indicated st 2 rows below, yo, pull up a loop (3 loops on hook), (yo, pull through 2 loops on hook) twice.

2 raised double crochet together (rdc2tog): yo, insert hook under 2 front strands of leg of indicated st 2 rows below, yo, pull up a loop (3 loops on hook), yo, pull through 2 loops on hook; yo, insert hook under 2 front strands of leg of next indicated st 2 rows below, yo, pull up a loop (4 loops on hook), yo, pull through 2 loops on hook (3 loops on hook), yo, pull through all 3 loops on hook at once. 1 st decreased.

Rdc worked in two front strands of the leg of sc two rows below.

Rdc worked around two front strands of leg of rdc two rows below.

LINEN RIB STITCH

Creates structured, vertical ribbing lines that add a clean, textured look on the right side, while the wrong side remains smooth and flat.

Note: *this pattern is worked over a multiple of 4 sts plus 1. Starting chains do not count as sts throughout.*

Start: Chain a multiple of 4 plus 2.

Row 1 (RS): 1 sc in back ridge (bump) of second ch from hook, 1 sc in back ridge (bump) of each ch to end. Turn.

Row 2: Ch 1, 2 sc, *ch 1, sk 1 st, 1 sc; rep from * to last st, 1 sc. Turn.

Row 3: Ch 1, 1 sc, ch 1, sk 1 st, 1 rdc, *ch 1, 1 sc, ch 1, 1 rdc; rep from * to last 2 sts, ch 1, sk 1 st, 1 sc. Turn.

Row 4: Ch 1, 2 sc, *ch 1, 1 sc; rep from * to last st, 1 sc. Turn.

Rep Rows 3 and 4 for pattern.

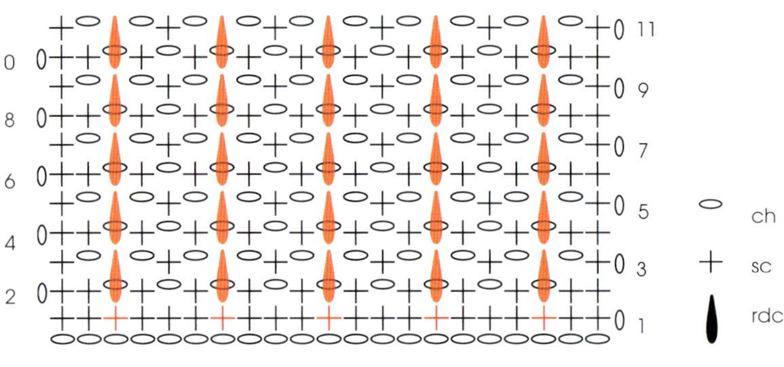

DIAGONAL DRIFT

Delicate rows of stacked diagonal lines give a gentle rhythm to the fabric.

Note: *this pattern is worked over a multiple of 4 sts plus 1. Starting chains do not count as sts throughout.*

Start: Chain a multiple of 4 plus 2.

Row 1 (RS): 1 sc in back ridge (bump) of second ch from hook, 1 sc in back ridge (bump) of each ch to end. Turn.

Row 2: Ch 1, 1 sc, *ch 1, sk 1 st, 1 sc; rep from * to end. Turn.

Row 3: Ch 1, 1 sc, 1 sc, ch 1, 1 rdc under ch-sp just worked, *ch 1, 1 sc, ch 1, 1 rdc in sc under ch-sp just worked; rep from * to last st, 1 sc. Turn.

Row 4: Ch 1, 1 sc, *ch 1, 1 sc; rep from * to last st, ch 1, 1 sc. Turn.

Rep Rows 3 and 4 for pattern.

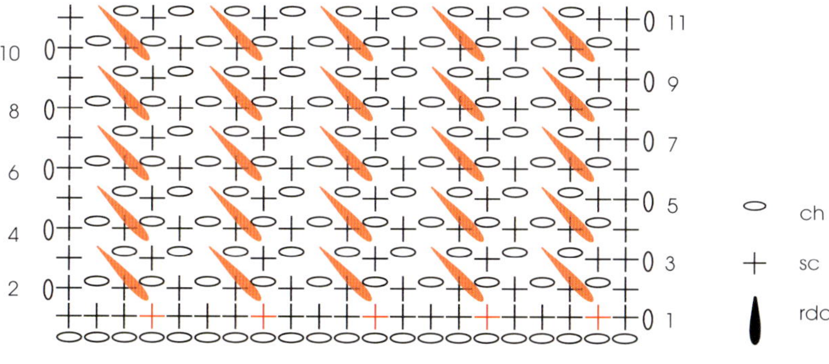

ARROWHEAD STITCH

Vertical rows of open V motifs give an airy lightness and rhythm to this textured fabric.

Note: *this pattern is worked over a multiple of 8 sts plus 7. Starting chains do not count as sts throughout.*

Start: Chain a multiple of 8.

Row 1 (RS): 1 sc in back ridge (bump) of second ch from hook, 1 sc in back ridge (bump) of each ch to end. Turn.

Row 2: Ch 1, 1 sc, *ch 1, sk 1 st, 1 sc; rep from * to end. Turn.

Row 3: Ch 1, 1 sc, 1 sc, ch 1, 1 rdc, *(ch 1, 1 sc) 3 times, ch 1, 1 rdc; rep from * to last ch-sp, ch 1, 1 sc in last ch-sp, 1 sc in last st. Turn.

Row 4: Ch 1, 1 sc, *ch 1, 1 sc; rep from * to last 2 sts, ch 1, sk 1 st, 1 sc. Turn.

Row 5: Ch 1, 1 sc, 1 rdc into next rdc, ch 1, 1 sc in ch-sp above rdc just worked, ch 1, 1 rdc in same rdc, *ch 1, 1 sc, ch 1, 1 rdc in next rdc, ch 1, 1 sc in ch-sp above rdc just worked, ch 1, 1 rdc in same rdc; rep from * to last st, 1 sc. Turn.

Row 6: Rep Row 4.

Rep Rows 3–6 for pattern.

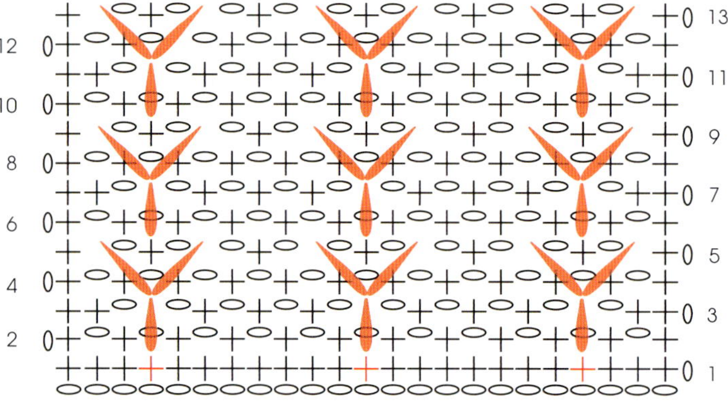

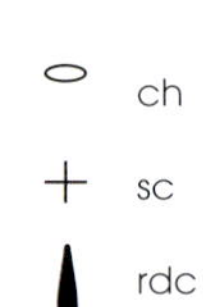

VINE CABLE STITCH

The vertical rows of closely spaced V and inverted V shapes create a textured, squishy fabric.

Note: *this pattern is worked over a multiple of 12 sts plus 1. Starting chains do not count as sts throughout.*

Start: Chain a multiple of 12 plus 2.

Row 1 (RS): 1 sc in back ridge (bump) of second ch from hook, 1 sc in back ridge (bump) of each ch to end. Turn.

Row 2: Ch 1, 1 sc, *ch 1, sk 1 st, 1 sc; rep from * to end. Turn.

Row 3: Ch 1, *1 sc, sk 1 ch-sp, 1 rdc under next ch-sp, ch 1, 1 sc in ch-sp above rdc just worked, ch 1, 1 rdc in same st, ch 1, 1 sc, ch 1, 1 rdc2tog under ch-sp just worked and following second ch-sp, ch 1; rep from * to last ch-sp, 1sc in last ch-sp,1 sc. Turn.

Row 4: Ch 1, 1 sc, *ch 1, 1 sc; rep from * to last st, ch 1, 1 sc. Turn.

Rep Rows 3 and 4 for pattern.

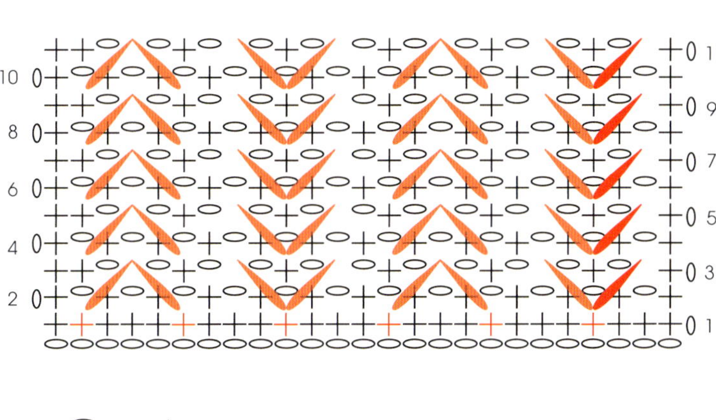

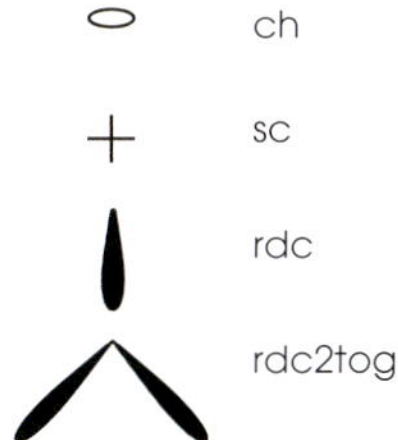

SPRIG STITCH

Bold, sweeping V shapes resemble branches reaching skywards, adding a nature-inspired texture to the fabric.

Note: *this pattern is worked over a multiple of 12 sts plus 1. Starting chains do not count as sts throughout.*

Start: Chain a multiple of 12 plus 2.

Row 1 (RS): 1 sc in back ridge (bump) of second ch from hook, 1 sc in back ridge (bump) of each ch to end. Turn.

Row 2 (WS): Ch 1, 2 sc, *ch 1, sk 1 st, 1 sc; rep from * to last st, 1 sc. Turn.

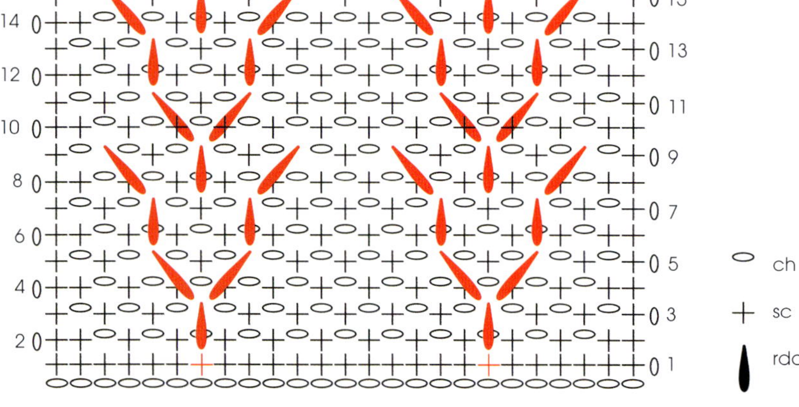

Row 3: Ch 1, 1 sc, (ch 1, 1 sc) twice, ch 1, 1 rdc, *ch 1, (1 sc, ch 1) 5 times, 1 rdc; rep from * to last 2 ch-sps, (ch 1, 1 sc) twice, ch 1, sk 1 st, 1 sc in last st. Turn.

Row 4 and all following WS rows: Ch 1, 2 sc, *ch 1, 1 sc; rep from * to last st, 1 sc. Turn.

Row 5: Ch 1, 1 sc, ch 1, 1 sc, ch 1, 1 rdc in next rdc, ch 1, 1 sc in ch-sp above rdc just worked, ch 1, 1 rdc in same rdc, *ch 1, (1 sc, ch 1) twice, 1 sc, 1 rdc in next rdc, ch 1, 1 sc in ch-sp above rdc just worked, ch 1, 1 rdc in same rdc; rep from * to last ch-sp, ch 1, 1 sc in last ch-sp, ch 1, sk 1 st, 1 sc. Turn.

Row 7: Ch 1, 1 sc, ch 1, 1 sc, ch 1, 1 rdc, ch 1, 1 sc, ch 1, 1 rdc, *(ch 1, 1 sc) 3 times, ch 1, 1 rdc, ch 1, 1 sc, ch 1, 1 rdc; rep from * to last ch-sp, ch 1, 1 sc in last ch-sp, ch 1, sk 1 st, 1 sc. Turn.

Row 9: Ch 1, 1 sc, ch 1, 1 rdc in next rdc, ch 1, 1 sc in ch-sp above rdc just worked, ch 1, 1 rdc, ch 1, 1 sc, ch 1, 1 rdc under ch-sp just worked, *ch 1, 1 sc, ch 1, 1 rdc in next rdc, ch 1, 1 sc in ch-sp above rdc just worked, ch 1, 1 rdc, ch 1, 1 sc, ch 1, 1 rdc under ch-sp just worked; rep from * to last 2 sts, ch 1, sk 1 st, 1 sc. Turn.

Row 10: Rep Row 4.

Rep Rows 5–10 for pattern.

SWEETHEART STITCH

Simple colorwork creates a playful grid of tiny hearts, perfect for heartfelt projects.

Note: *this pattern is worked over a multiple of 4 sts plus 3. Starting chains do not count as sts throughout.*

Start: With MC, chain a multiple of 4.

Row 1 (RS): 1 sc in back ridge (bump) of second ch from hook, 1 sc in back ridge (bump) of each ch to end. Turn.

Row 2: Ch 1, 1 sc, *ch 1, sk 1 st, 1 sc; rep from * to end. Turn.

Change to CC.

Row 3: Ch 1, 1 sc, 1 rdc, *ch 1, 1 sc, ch 1, 1 rdc; rep from * to last st, 1 sc. Turn.

Row 4: Ch 1, 1 sc, *ch 1, 1 sc; rep from * to last st, ch 1, 1 sc. Turn.

Change to MC.

Row 5: Ch 1, 2 sc, *ch 1, 1 sc; rep from * to last st, 1 sc. Turn.

Row 6: Rep Row 4.

Change to CC.

Row 7: Ch 1, 2 sc, ch 1, 1 rdc, *ch 1, 1 sc, ch 1, 1 rdc; rep from * to last ch-sp, ch 1, 1 sc in last ch-sp, 1 sc in last st. Turn.

Row 8: Rep Row 4.

Change to MC.

Rows 9 and 10: Rep Rows 5 and 6.

Repeat Rows 3–10 for pattern, changing colors every 2 rows.

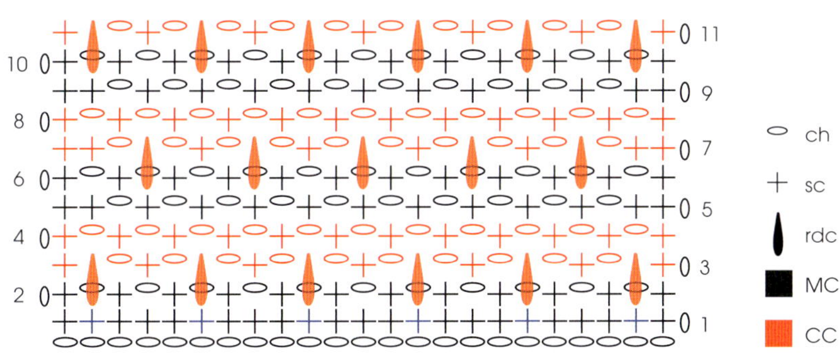

Change to next color on the last yo of the previous stitch.

DOTTED STRIPES STITCH

Alternating the colors and placement of rdc stitches in this pattern creates a structured, rhythmic colorwork effect.

Note: *this pattern is worked over a multiple of 4 sts plus 3. Starting chains do not count as sts throughout.*

Start: With MC, chain a multiple of 4.

Row 1 (RS): 1 sc in back ridge (bump) of second ch from hook, 1 sc in back ridge (bump) of each ch to end. Turn.

Row 2: Ch 1, 1 sc, *ch 1, sk 1 st, 1 sc; rep from * to end. Turn.

Change to CC.

Row 3: Ch 1, 1 sc, 1 rdc, *ch 1, 1 sc, ch 1, 1 rdc; rep from * to last st, 1 sc. Turn.

Row 4: Ch 1, 1 sc, *ch 1, 1 sc; rep from * to last st, ch 1, 1 sc. Turn.

Change to MC.

Row 5: Ch 1, 1 sc, *1 sc i, ch 1, 1 rdc, ch 1; rep from * to last ch-sp, 1 sc in last ch-sp, 1 sc in last st. Turn.

Row 6: Rep Row 4.

Rep Rows 3–6 for pattern changing colors every 2 rows.

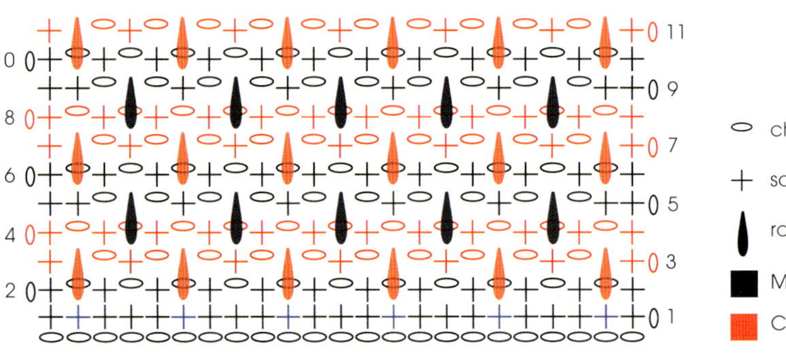

Change to next color on the last yo of the previous stitch.

FLAME STITCH

Staggered pattern repeats in alternating colors combine to create a series of flame-like motifs.

Note: *this pattern is worked over a multiple of 4 sts plus 3. Starting chains do not count as sts throughout.*

Start: With MC, chain a multiple of 4.

Row 1 (RS): 1 sc in back ridge (bump) of second ch from hook, 1 sc in back ridge (bump) of each ch to end. Turn.

Row 2: Ch 1, 1 sc, *ch 1, sk 1 st, 1 sc; rep from * to end. Turn.

Change to CC.

Row 3: Ch 1, 1 sc, 1 rdc, *ch 1, 1 sc, ch 1, 1 rdc; rep from * to last st, 1 sc. Turn.

Row 4: Ch 1, 1 sc, *ch 1, 1 sc; rep from * to last 2 sts, ch 1, sk 1 st, 1 sc. Turn.

Change to MC.

Rows 5 and 6: Rep Rows 3 and 4.

Change to CC.

Row 7: Ch 1, 1 sc, *1 sc, ch 1, 1 rdc, ch 1; rep from * to last ch-sp, ch 1, 1 sc in last ch-sp, 1 sc in last st. Turn.

Row 8: Rep Row 4.

Change to MC.

Rows 9 and 10: Rep Rows 7 and 8.

Rep Rows 3–10 for pattern, changing colors every 2 rows.

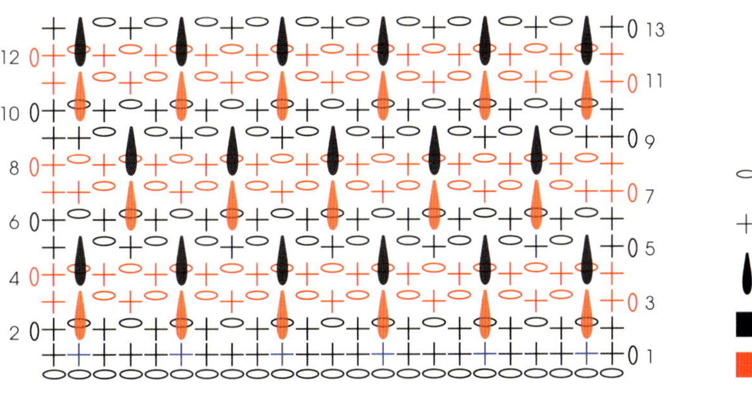

Change to next color on the last yo of the previous stitch.

FLOWERBED STITCH

Rows of plain linen stitch combine with rows of staggered rdc stitches, creating a cheerful pattern resembling an ornamental flowerbed.

Note: *this pattern is worked over a multiple of 4 sts plus 3. Starting chains do not count as sts throughout.*

Start: Using MC, chain a multiple of 4.

Row 1 (RS): 1 sc in back ridge (bump) of second ch from hook, 1 sc in back ridge (bump) of each ch to end. Turn.

Row 2 (WS): Ch 1, 1 sc, *ch 1, sk 1 st, 1 sc; rep from * to end. Turn.

Change to CC.

Row 3: Ch 1, 1 sc, 1 sc, *ch 1, 1 sc; rep from * to last st, 1 sc. Turn.

Row 4: Ch 1, 1 sc, *ch 1, 1 sc; rep from * to last 2 sts, ch 1, sk 1 st, 1 sc. Turn.

Change to MC.

Row 5: Ch 1, 1 sc, 1 rdc, *ch 1, 1 sc, ch 1, 1 rdc; rep from * to last st, 1 sc. Turn.

Row 6: Rep Row 4.

Change to CC.

Row 7: Ch 1, 1 sc, 1 sc, ch 1, 1 rdc, *ch 1, 1 sc, ch 1, 1 rdc; rep from * to last ch-sp, ch 1, 1 sc in last ch-sp, 1 sc in last st. Turn.

Row 8: Rep Row 4.

Change to MC.

Rows 9 and 10: Rep Rows 3 and 4.

Rep Rows 3–10 for pattern, changing colors every 2 rows.

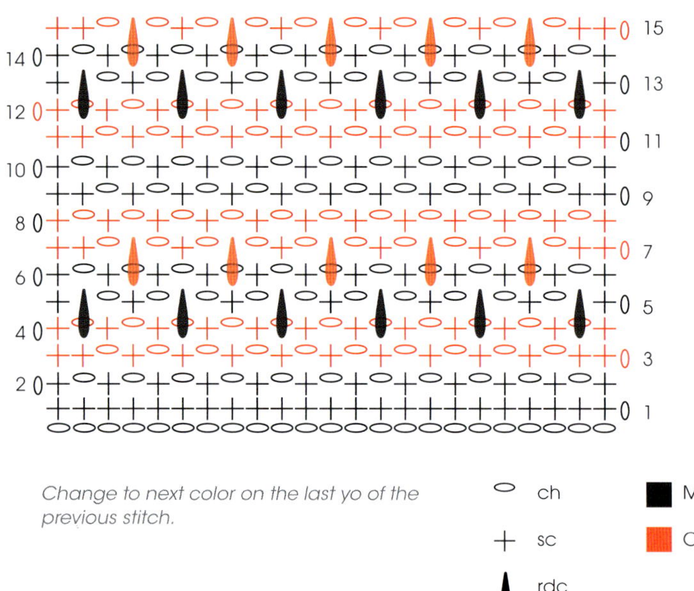

Change to next color on the last yo of the previous stitch.

STARDUST STITCH

The diagonal placement of the rdc sts create an elongated diamond pattern that resembles falling stars.

Note: *this pattern is worked over a multiple of 8 sts plus 5. Starting chains do not count as sts throughout.*

Start: With MC, chain a multiple of 8 plus 6.

Row 1 (RS): 1 sc in back ridge (bump) of second ch from hook, 1 sc in back ridge (bump) of each ch to end. Turn.

Row 2: Ch 1, 1 sc, *ch 1, sk 1 st, 1 sc; rep from * to end. Turn.

Change to CC.

Row 3: Ch 1, 1 sc, ch 1, 1 rdc, *(ch 1, 1 sc) 3 times, ch 1, 1 rdc; rep from * to last 2 sts, ch 1, sk 1 st, 1 sc. Turn.

Row 4: Ch 1, 1 sc, 1 sc, *ch 1, 1 sc; rep from * to last st, 1 sc. Turn.

Change to MC.

Row 5: Ch 1, 1 sc, ch 1, sk 1 ch-sp, 1 rdc under next ch-sp, (ch 1, 1 sc) 3 times, ch 1, *1 rdc2tog under ch-sp just worked and following second ch-sp, (ch 1, 1 sc) 3 times, ch 1; rep from * to last ch-sp, 1 rdc under ch-sp just worked, ch 1, sk last ch-sp and next st, 1 sc in last st. Turn.

Row 6: Rep Row 4.

Change to CC.

Row 7: Ch 1, 1 sc, (ch 1, 1 sc) twice, ch 1, 1 rdc, *(ch 1, 1 sc) 3 times, ch 1, 1 rdc; rep from * to last 2 ch-sps, (ch 1, 1 sc) twice, ch 1, sk 1 st, 1 sc. Turn.

Row 8: Rep Row 4.

Change to MC.

Row 9: Ch 1, 1 sc, (ch 1, 1 sc) twice, ch 1, *rdc2tog under ch-sp just worked and following second ch-sp, ch 1, 1 sc in ch-sp above rdc just worked, (ch 1, 1 sc) twice, ch 1; rep from * to end, working last sc on final repeat into last st of row instead of ch-sp. Turn.

Row 10: Rep Row 4.

Rep Rows 3–10 for pattern, changing colors every 2 rows.

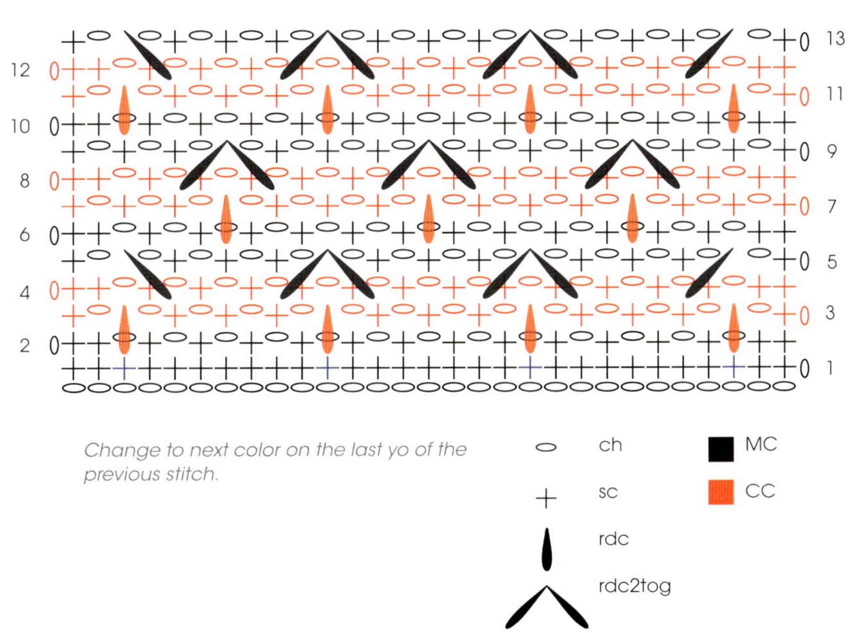

Change to next color on the last yo of the previous stitch.

LINEN STITCH PROJECT

Golden Hour Shawl

Golden Hour is a cozy shawl that gently brightens any moment, much like the golden light just before sunset.

Increases at the end of each row create a lovely, comfy boomerang shape that wraps beautifully around the shoulders. The shawl is also easily adjustable – just add more rows to make a larger shawl.

Three different stitch patterns and two colors provide plenty of variation: the first section is softly textured, and followed by playful colorwork, which is beautifully offset by bold ribbing along the edge.

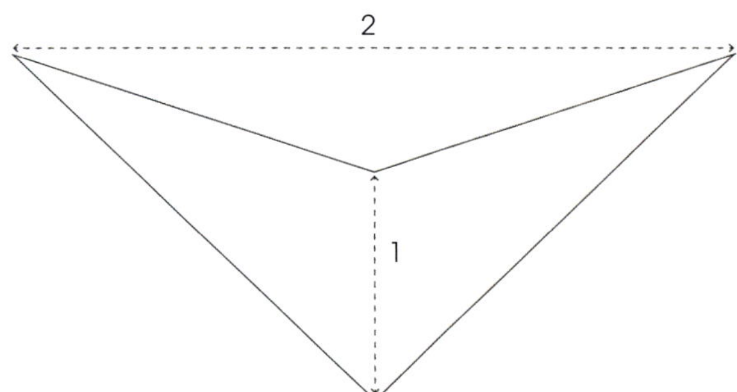

YOU WILL NEED

YARN

Malabrigo Sock (100% superwash Merino wool), 3-ply/light fingering, 100g (402m/440yds), in the following shades:

Main color (MC): Natural (SW063); 1 skein

Contrast color (CC): Frank Ochre (SW035); 1 skein

HOOKS

Size 3.5mm (US E/4) hook

TENSION

26 sts (sc and ch-sp) and 22 rows measure 10 x 10cm (4 x 4in) over Linen st using a 3.5mm (US E/4) hook.

MEASUREMENTS

Depth (1): 47cm (18½in)

Wingspan (2): 134cm (52¾in)

ABBREVIATIONS

CC	contrast color
ch	chain
ch-sp	chain space
MC	main color
rep	repeat
RS	right side of work
sc	single crochet
sk	skip/miss
sp	space
st(s)	stitch(es)
tr	treble crochet
WS	wrong side of work
yo	yarn over

SPECIAL STITCHES

Raised double crochet (rdc) (See Chapter 2: Special Stitches)

Extended single crochet (esc) (See Chapter 1: Special Stitches)

INSTRUCTIONS

BODY

Using MC, make a magic ring.

Row 1 (WS): Ch 1 (does not count as a st), 5 sc into ring. Turn. (5 sts).

Row 2 (RS): Ch 1, (1 sc, ch 1, 1 sc) in first st, ch 1, sk 1 st, (1 sc, ch 2, 1 sc) in next st, ch 1, sk 1 st, (1 sc, 1 esc) in last st. Turn. (6 sts, 4 ch-sps)

Note: *the shawl continues in linen st. Only the first and last sts of each row are worked into, and all other sts are worked into the ch-sps. Rdc sts are worked into the st 2 rows below the next ch-sp.*

Row 3: Ch 1, (1 sc, ch 1, 1 sc) in first st, ch 1, 1 sc, ch 1, (1 sc, ch 2, 1 sc) in ch2-sp, (ch 1, 1 sc) twice, ch 1, (1 sc, 1 esc) in last st. Turn. (9 sts, 7 ch-sp)

Row 4: Ch 1, (1 sc, ch 1, 1 sc) in first st, (ch 1, 1 sc) twice, ch 1, 1 rdc, ch 1, (1 sc, ch 2, 1 sc) in ch2-sp, ch 1, 1 rdc, (ch 1, 1 sc) twice, ch 1, (1 sc, 1 esc) in last st. Turn. (12 sts, 10 ch-sp)

Row 5: Ch 1, (1 sc, ch 1, 1 sc) in first st, *ch 1, 1 sc; rep from * to ch2-sp, ch 1, (1 sc, ch 2, 1 sc) in ch2-sp, *ch 1, 1 sc; rep from * to last st, ch 1, (1 sc, 1 esc) in last st. Turn. (3 sts and 3 ch-sp increased)

Row 6: Ch 1, (1 sc, ch 1, 1 sc) in first st, *ch 1, 1 sc, ch 1, 1 rdc; rep from * to ch2-sp, ch 1, (1 sc, ch 2, 1 sc) in ch2-sp, ch 1, **1 rdc, ch 1, 1 sc, ch 1; rep from ** to last st, (1 sc, 1 esc) in last st. Turn. (3 sts and 3 ch-sp increased)

Row 7: Rep Row 5. (3 sts and 3 ch-sp increased)

Row 8: Ch 1, (1 sc, ch 1, 1 sc) in first st, ch 1, 1 sc, *ch 1, 1 sc, ch 1, 1 rdc; rep from * to ch2-sp, ch 1, (1 sc, ch 2, 1 sc) in ch2-sp, ch 1, **1 rdc, ch 1, 1 sc, ch 1; rep from ** to last ch-sp, ch 1, 1 sc, ch 1, (1 sc, 1 esc) in last st. Turn. (3 sts and 3 ch-sp increased)

Row 9: Rep Row 5. (3 sts and 3 ch-sp increased)

Rows 10–53: Rep Rows 6–9 another 11 times. (159 sts, 157 ch-sps)

COLORWORK

Change to CC.

Rows 54 and 55: Rep Row 5 twice. (165 sts, 163 ch-sps)

Change to MC.

Rows 56 and 57: Rep Row 5 twice. (171 sts, 169 ch-sps)

Change to CC.

Rows 58 and 59: Rep Row 5 twice. (177 sts, 175 ch-sps)

Change to MC.

Row 60: Ch 1, (1 sc, ch 1, 1 sc) in first st, ch 1, 1 sc, ch 1, *1 rdc, ch 1, 1 sc, ch 1; rep from * to ch2-sp, 1 sc in ch2-sp, 1 tr in ch2-sp 2 rows below, 1 sc in ch2-sp, ch 1, 1 sc, ch 1, **1 rdc, ch 1, 1 sc, ch 1; rep from ** to last ch-sp, 1 sc, ch 1, (1 sc, 1 esc) in last st. Turn. (4 sts including 1 tr, and 2 ch-sp increased)

Row 61: Ch 1, (1 sc, ch 1, 1 sc) in first st, *ch 1, 1 sc; rep from * to corner tr, ch 1, (1 sc, ch 2, 1 sc) in tr, **ch 1, 1 sc; rep from ** to last st, ch 1, (1 sc, 1 esc) in last st. Turn. (2 sts and 4 ch-sp increased)

Change to CC.

Row 62: Ch 1, (1 sc, ch 1, 1 sc) in first st, (ch 1, 1 sc) twice, ch 1, *1 rdc, ch 1, 1 sc, ch 1; rep from * to ch2-sp, ch 1, (1 sc, ch 2, 1 sc) in ch2-sp, ch 1, 1 sc, ch 1, **1 rdc, ch 1, 1 sc, ch 1; rep from ** to last ch-sp, ch 1, 1 sc, ch 1, (1 sc, 1 esc) in last st. Turn. (3 sts and 3 ch-sp increased)

Row 63: Rep Row 5. (3 sts and 3 ch-sp increased)

Change to MC.

Rows 64 and 65: Rep Row 5. (195 sts, 193 ch-sp)

Change to CC.

Rows 66 and 67: Rep Row 5. (201 sts, 199 ch-sp)

Change to MC.

Rows 68 and 69: Rep Rows 60 and 61. (207 sts, 205 ch-sp)

Fasten off MC. Continue with CC.

Rows 70 and 71: Rep Rows 62 and 63. (213 sts, 211 ch-sp)

RIBBING

Row 72: Rep Row 6. (216 sts, 214 ch-sp)

Row 73: Rep Row 5. (219 sts, 207 ch-sps)

Row 74: Ch 1, (1 sc, ch 1, 1 sc) in first st, *ch 1, 1 sc, ch 1, 1 rdc; rep from * to ch2-sp, ch 1, (1 sc, ch 2, 1 sc) in ch2-sp, ch 1, **1 rdc, ch 1, 1 sc, ch 1; rep from ** to last 2 ch-sps, 1 rdc, ch 1, 1 sc, ch 1, (1 sc, 1 esc) in last st. Turn. (222 sts, 220 ch-sp)

Row 75: Rep Row 5. (225 sts, 223 ch-sp)

Row 76: Ch 1, (1 sc, ch 1, 1 sc) in first st, ch 1, 1 sc, ch 1, *1 rdc, ch 1, sc, ch 1; rep from * to ch2-sp, (1 sc, ch 2, 1 sc) in ch2-sp, **ch 1, 1 sc, ch 1, 1 rdc; rep from ** to last ch-sp, ch 1, 1 sc, ch 1, (1 sc, 1 esc) in last st. Turn. (228 sts, 226 ch-sp)

Rows 77–84: Rep Rows 73–76 twice more. (252 sts, 250 ch-sp)

Fasten off.

FINISHING

Wet block your shawl to the finished measurements. Lay the wet shawl out on a flat surface. Align the edges to given dimensions (note that the wingspan is not a straight line). Let it dry completely.

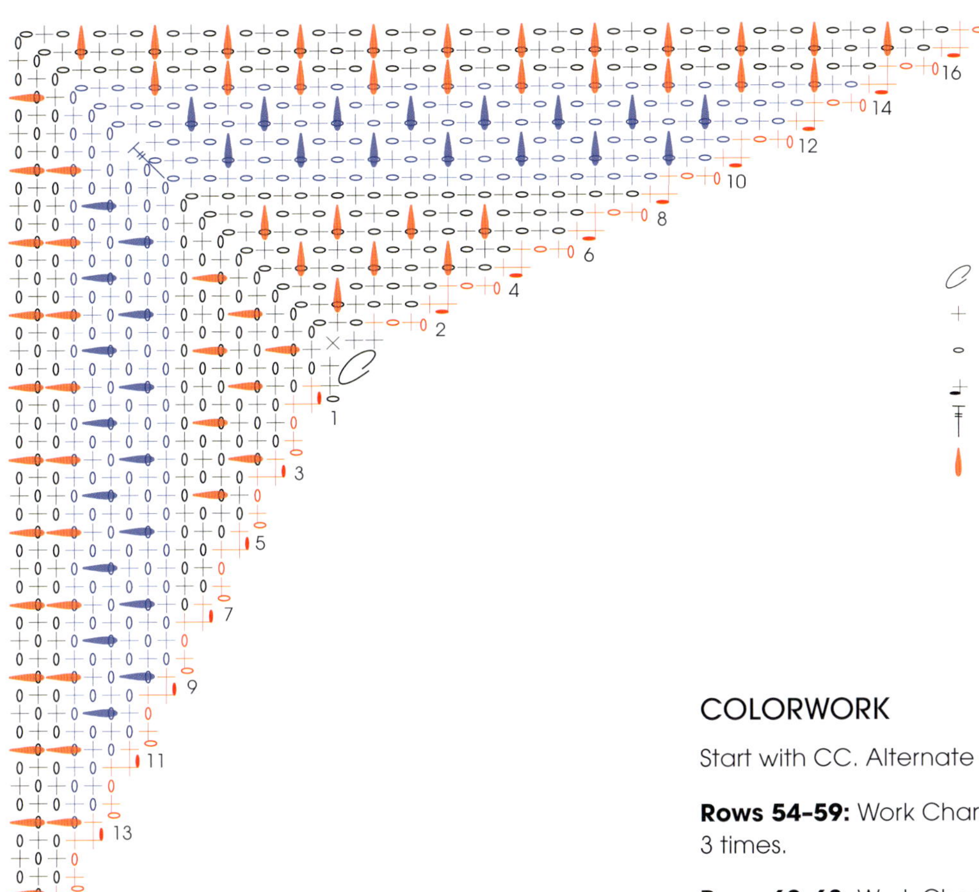

CHART INSTRUCTIONS

The simplified chart includes all three sections of the shawl: Body (Chart rows 1–9), Colorwork (Chart Rows 10–15) and Ribbing (Chart Rows 16–18).

BODY

Start with MC.

Rows 1-9: Work Chart Rows 1–9.

Rows 10-53: Rep Chart Rows 6–9 another 11 times.

COLORWORK

Start with CC. Alternate colors every 2 rows.

Rows 54-59: Work Chart Rows 10 and 11 a total of 3 times.

Rows 60-63: Work Chart Rows 12–15 once.

Rows 64-67: Rep Chart Rows 10 and 11 twice more.

Rows 68-71: Rep Chart Rows 12–15 once more.

Break MC and continue with CC only.

RIBBING

Rows 72-74: Work Chart Rows 16–18.

Row 75: Rep Chart Row 17 once more.

Rows 76-83: Rep last 4 rows twice more.

Row 84: Rep Chart Row 16.

FINISHING

See written instructions.

CHAPTER 3:

TEXTURE, LACE, AND COLORWORK

This chapter uses single crochet back-loop ribbing as a foundation, and embellishes it with various combinations of stitches including eyelets, stars, circles, and diamonds. Inspired by the fluidity of nature, these patterns capture the gentle movement of water, the rise and fall of waves, and the soft shapes of drifting clouds.

Some of the stitch patterns in this chapter feature a simple but ingenious technique that shapes the ribbing ridges around other shapes without interrupting their flow. This creates a stunning effect, especially when worked in multiple colors.

Together, these patterns bring a sense of gentle motion and depth to your fabric, transforming simple ribbing into a vibrant, textured landscape.

STITCH FOCUS:

Twisted single crochet (X-sc)

NOTES ON TECHNIQUE

In all stitch patterns based on single-crochet ribbing, work the last stitch of each row into both loops to prevent the edge from stretching.

SPECIAL STITCHES

In this chapter, you'll discover a new stitch, the X-sc – a variation of the regular sc2tog that twists the stitches to create neatly rounded, tiny eyelets.

X-sc: Sk 1 st and insert hook in FLO of next st (A), yo, pull up a loop (2 loops on hook). Insert hook in FLO of skipped st from back to front (B), yo, pull up a loop (3 loops on hook), yo, pull through all 3 loops on hook (C).

Insert the hook into front loop of next st.

Insert the hook in front loop of skipped stitch from back to front.

Pull through all three loops on the hook.

MINI EYELET RIDGE STITCH

Rows of single-crochet ribbing are enlivened with tiny, perfectly rounded eyelets. The alternating ribbing and eyelets give the fabric a structured yet airy texture.

Note: *this pattern is worked over a multiple of 2 sts. Starting chains do not count as sts throughout.*

Start: Chain a multiple of 2 plus 1.

Row 1 (WS): 1 sc in back ridge (bump) of second ch from hook, 1 sc in back ridge (bump) of each ch to end. Turn.

Row 2: Ch 1, 1 sc BLO in each st to last st, 1 sc. Turn.

Row 3: Ch 1, 1 sc, ch 1, *1 X-sc over next 2 sts, ch 1; rep from * to last st, 1 sc. Turn.

Row 4: Ch 1, 1 sc, 1 sc in next ch-sp, *2 sc in next ch-sp; rep from * to last ch-sp, 1 sc in last ch-sp, 1 sc. Turn.

Rows 5 and 6: Rep Row 2.

Rep Rows 3–6 for pattern.

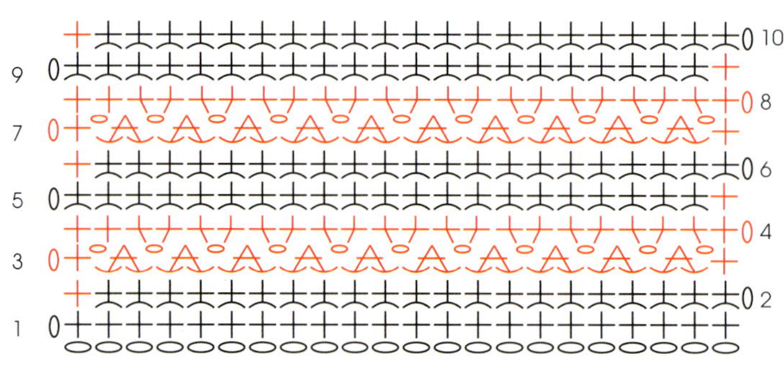

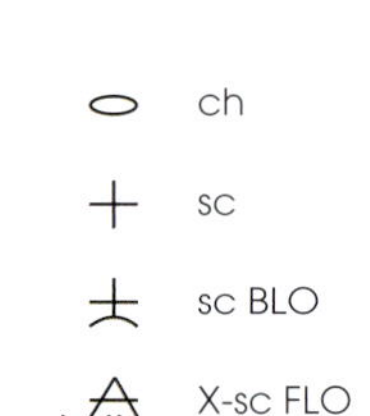

OPEN RIDGE LACE STITCH

Large, bold eyelets nestle between rows of simple single-crochet ribbing, creating a generous, open texture that's full of fun.

Note: *this pattern is worked over a multiple of 7 sts plus 6. Starting chains do not count as sts throughout.*

Start: Chain a multiple of 7.

Row 1 (WS): 1 sc in back ridge (bump) of second ch from hook, 1 sc in back ridge (bump) of each ch to end. Turn.

Row 2: Ch 1, 1 sc BLO in each st to last st, 1 sc. Turn.

Row 3: Ch 1, 1 sc BLO, 1 sc, *ch 4, sk 2 sts, 1 sc, 3 sc BLO, 1 sc; rep from * to last 4 sts, ch 4, sk 2 sts, 2 sc. Turn.

Row 4: Ch 1, sc2tog BLO, *5 sc in ch4-sp, sc2tog BLO, 1 sc BLO, sc2tog BLO; rep from * to last ch-sp, 5 sc in last ch4-sp, sc2tog in BLO of next st and both loops of last st. Turn.

Row 5: Rep Row 2.

Row 6: Ch 1, 7 sc BLO, *sk 1 st, 7 sc BLO; rep from * to last 8 sts, sk 1 st, 6 sc BLO, 1 sc. Turn.

Row 7: Ch 1, 5 sc BLO, 1 sc, *ch 4, sk 2 sts, 1 sc, 3 sc BLO, 1 sc; rep from * to last 8 sts, ch 4, sk 2 sts, 1 sc, 4 sc BLO, 1 sc. Turn.

Row 8: Ch 1, 1 sc, sc2tog BLO, 1 sc BLO, sc2tog BLO, *5 sc in ch4-sp, sc2tog BLO, 1 sc BLO, sc2tog BLO; rep from * to last st, 1 sc. Turn.

Row 9: Rep Row 2.

Row 10: Ch 1, 10 sc BLO, *sk 1 st, 7 sc BLO; rep from * to last 3 sts, 2 sc BLO, 1 sc. Turn.

Rep Rows 3–10 for pattern.

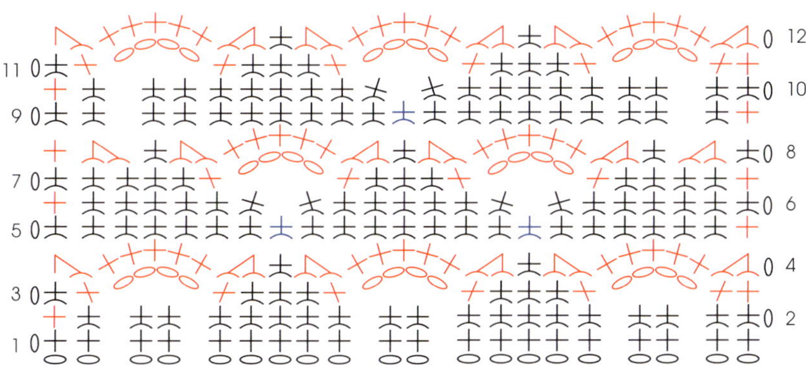

ch
sc
sc BLO
sc2tog BLO
sc2tog in BLO of 1 st and both loops of next st

DAISY-CHAIN RIDGE STITCH

This simple single-crochet ribbing is sprinkled with tiny star stitches in an even pattern, creating a daisy-chain effect that adds charm and extra texture to the fabric.

Note: *this pattern is worked over a multiple of 8 sts. Starting chains do not count as sts throughout.*

Start: Chain a multiple of 8 plus 1.

Row 1 (WS): 1 sc in back ridge (bump) of second ch from hook, 1 sc in back ridge (bump) of each ch to end. Turn.

Row 2: Ch 1, 1 sc BLO in each st to last st, 1 sc. Turn.

Row 3 (WS): Ch 1, 3 sc BLO, *3-spike Star-st, 6 sc BLO; rep from * to last 5 sts, 3-spike Star-st, 2 sc BLO, 1 sc. Turn.

Row 4 (RS): Ch 1, 3 sc BLO, *2 hdc in top of Star-st, 6 sc BLO; rep from * to last Star-st, 2 hdc in top of last Star-st, 2 sc BLO, 1 sc. Turn.

Rows 5 and 6: Rep Row 2.

Row 7: Ch 1, 7 sc BLO, *3-spike Star-st, 6 sc BLO; rep from * to last st, 1 sc. Turn.

Row 8: Ch 1, 7 sc BLO, *2 hdc in top of Star-st, 6 sc BLO; rep from * to last Star-st, 2 hdc in top of last Star-st, 2 sc BLO, 1 sc. Turn.

Rows 9 and 10: Rep Row 2.

Rep Rows 3–10 for pattern.

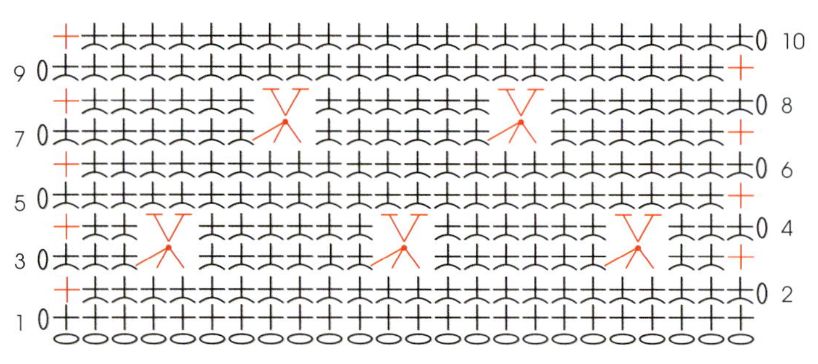

- ch
- sc
- sc BLO
- 3-spike Star-st
- hdc
- 2 hdc in same st

FULL CIRCLE RIDGE STITCH

Combining single-crochet ribbing with the classic Catherine wheel design creates bold, textured circles outlined by raised ridges.

Note: *this pattern is worked over a multiple of 12 sts plus 2. Starting chains do not count as sts unless specified.*

Start: Chain a multiple of 12 plus 3.

Row 1 (WS): 1 sc in back ridge (bump) of second ch from hook, 1 sc in back ridge (bump) of each ch to end. Turn.

Row 2: Ch 1, 1 sc BLO in each st to last st, 1 sc. Turn.

Row 3: Ch 3 (counts as 1 dc), sk first st, dc4tog, *ch 2, 5 sc BLO, ch 3, dc7tog; rep from * to last 10 sts, ch 2, 5 sc BLO, ch 3, dc4tog, 1 dc. Turn.

Row 4: Ch 3 (counts as 1 dc), sk first st, 4 dc in dc4tog, 5 sc BLO, *7 dc in next dc7tog, 5 sc BLO; rep from * to last dc4tog, 4 dc in dc4tog, 1 dc. Turn.

Rows 5 and 6: Rep Row 2.

Row 7: Ch 1, 4 sc BLO, ch 2, dc7tog, ch 3, 5 sc BLO; rep from * to last 11 sts, ch 2, dc7tog, ch 3, 3 sc BLO, 1 sc. Turn.

Row 8: Ch 1, 4 sc BLO, 7 dc in next dc7tog, 5 sc BLO sts, *7 dc in next dc7tog, 5 sc BLO; rep from * to last dc7tog, 7 dc in dc7tog, 3 sc BLO, 1 sc. Turn.

Rows 9 and 10: Rep Row 2.

Rep Rows 3–10 for pattern.

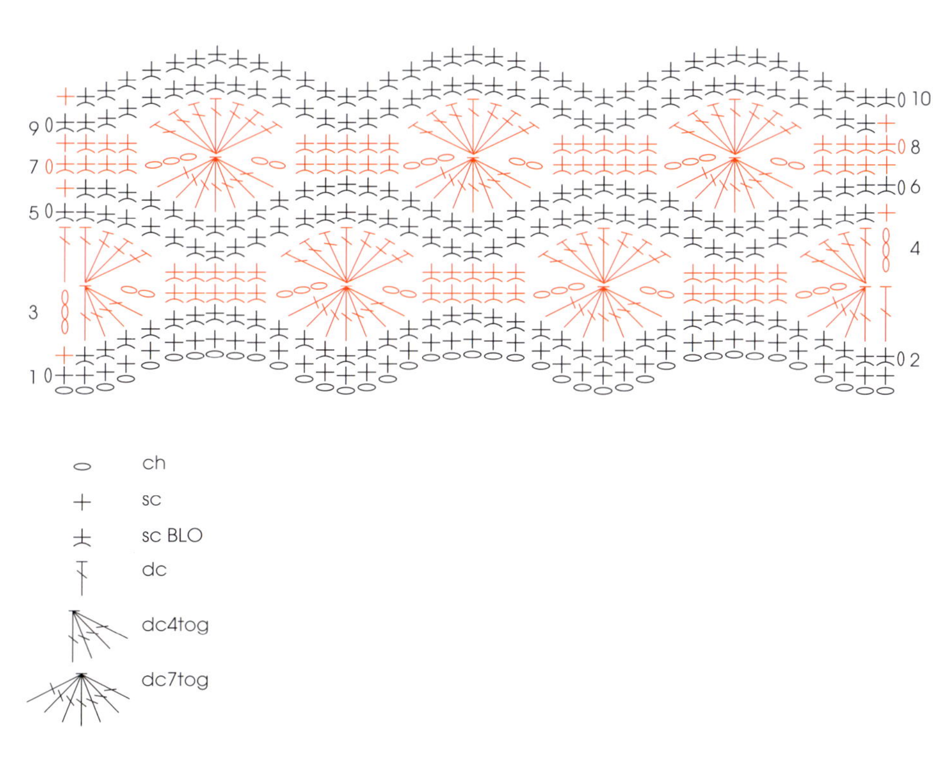

INTERRUPTED RIDGE STITCH

Back loop single crochet worked with skipped stitches creates an interesting, bubbly effect.

Note: *this pattern is worked over a multiple of 12 sts plus 7. Starting chains do not count as sts throughout.*

Start: Chain a multiple of 12 plus 8.

Row 1 (WS): 1 sc in back ridge (bump) of second ch from hook, 1 sc in back ridge (bump) of each ch to end. Turn.

Row 2: Ch 1, 1 sc BLO in each st to last st, 1 sc. Turn.

Row 3: Ch 1, *7 sc BLO, ch 5, sk 5 sts; rep from * to last 7 sts, 6 sc BLO, 1 sc. Turn.

Row 4: Ch 1, *7 sc BLO, ch 5, sk ch5-sp; rep from * to last 7 sts, 6 sc BLO, 1 sc. Turn.

Row 5: Ch 1, *7 sc BLO, 5 sc BLO in unworked sts 3 rows below (work behind ch5-sp); rep from * to last 7 sts, 6 sc BLO, 1 sc. Turn.

Row 6: Rep Row 2.

Rows 7–10: Rep Rows 3–6.

Row 11: Ch 1, 1 sc BLO, *ch 5, sk 5 sts, 7 sc BLO; rep from * to last 6 sts, ch 5, sk 5 sts,1 sc. Turn.

Row 12: Ch 1, 1 sc BLO, *ch 5, sk ch5-sp, 7 sc BLO; rep from * to last ch5-sp, ch 5, sk ch5-sp, 1 sc. Turn.

Row 13: Ch 1, 1 sc BLO, *5 sc BLO in unworked sts 3 rows below (work behind ch5-sp), 7 sc BLO; rep from * to last ch5-sp, 5 sc BLO in unworked sts 3 rows below (work behind ch5-sp), 1 sc. Turn.

Row 14: Rep Row 2.

Rows 15–18: Rep Rows 11–14.

Rep Rows 3–18 for pattern.

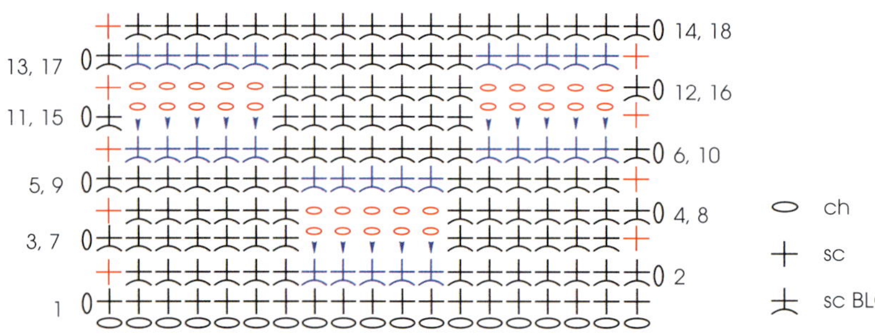

PEAPOD RIDGE STITCH

X-sc eyelets are combined with the technique used in the Interrupted Rib Stitch to create a series of almond-shaped motifs, giving the fabric a layered texture.

Note: *this pattern is worked over a multiple of 14 sts plus 8. Starting chains do not count as sts throughout.*

Start: Chain a multiple of 14 plus 9.

Row 1 (WS): 1 sc in back ridge (bump) of second ch from hook, 1 sc in back ridge (bump) of each ch to end. Turn.

Row 2: Ch 1, 1 sc BLO in each st to last st, 1 sc. Turn.

Row 3: Ch 1, 1 sc, (ch 1, 1 X-sc over next 2 sts) 3 times, ch 1, 1 sc, *ch 6, sk 6 sts, 1 sc, (ch 1, 1 X-sc over next 2 sts) 3 times, ch 1, 1 sc; rep from * to end. Turn.

Row 4: Ch 1, 1 sc, 1 sc in next ch-sp, (1 sc, 1 hdc) in next ch-sp, (1 hdc, 1 sc) in next ch-sp, 1 sc in next ch-sp, 1 sc, *ch 6, sk ch6-sp, 1 sc, 1 sc in next ch-sp, (1 sc, 1 hdc) in next ch-sp, (1 hdc, 1 sc) in next ch-sp, sk 1 st, 1 sc in next ch-sp, 1 sc; rep from * to end. Turn.

Row 5: Ch 1, *8 sc BLO, 6 sc BLO in unworked sts 3 rows below (work behind ch6-sp); rep from * to last 8 sts, 7 sc BLO, 1 sc. Turn.

Row 6: Rep Row 2.

Row 7: Ch 1, 1 sc, *ch 6, sk 6 sts, 1 sc, (ch 1, 1 X-sc over next 2 sts) 3 times, ch 1, 1 sc; rep from * to last 7 sts, ch 6, sk 6 sts, 1 sc. Turn.

Row 8: Ch 1, 1 sc, *ch 6, sk ch6-sp, 1 sc, 1 sc in next ch-sp, (1 sc, 1 hdc) in next ch-sp, (1 hdc, 1 sc) in next ch-sp, sk 1 st, 1 sc in next ch-sp, 1 sc; rep from * to last ch6-sp, ch 6, sk ch6-sp, 1 sc. Turn.

Row 9: Ch 1, 1 sc BLO, 6 sc BLO in unworked sts 3 rows below (work behind ch6-sp), *8 sc BLO, 6 sc BLO in unworked sts 3 rows below (work behind ch6-sp); rep from * to last st, 1 sc. Turn.

Row 10: Rep Row 2.

Rep Rows 3–10 for pattern.

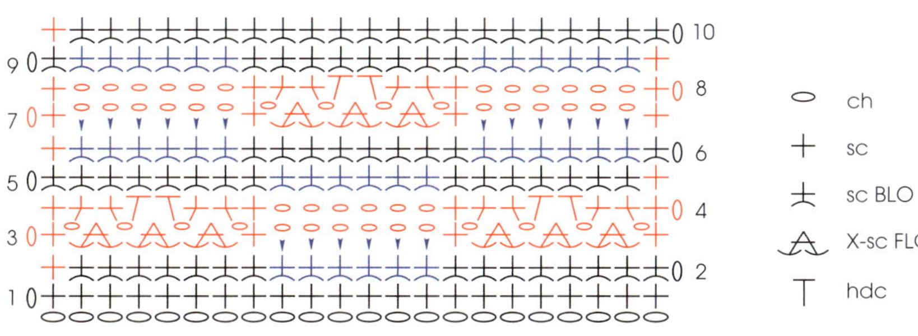

WATERLILY STITCH

Back loop single crochet combines beautifully with star stitches to form gentle waves and curves in the fabric.

Note: *this pattern is worked over a multiple of 14 sts plus 8. Starting chains do not count as sts throughout.*

Start: Chain a multiple of 14 plus 9.

Row 1 (WS): 1 sc in back ridge (bump) of second ch from hook, 1 sc in back ridge (bump) of each ch to end. Turn.

Row 2: Ch 1, 1 sc BLO in each st to last st, 1 sc. Turn.

Row 3: Ch 1, 1 sc, 2 sc BLO, 3-spike Star-st, 2 sc BLO, 1 sc, *ch 6, sk 6 sts, 1 sc, 2 sc BLO, 3-spike Star-st, 2 sc BLO, 1 sc; rep from * to end. Turn.

Row 4: Ch 1, *3 sc BLO, 2 hdc in top of Star-st, 3 sc BLO, ch 6, sk ch6-sp; rep to last 7 sts, 3 sc BLO, 2 hdc in top of Star-st, 2 sc BLO, 1 sc. Turn.

Row 5: Ch 1, *8 sc BLO, 6 sc BLO in unworked sts 3 rows below (work behind ch6-sp); rep from * to last 8 sts, 7 sc BLO, 1 sc. Turn.

Row 6: Rep Row 2.

Row 7: Ch 1, 1 sc, *ch 6, sk 6 sts, 1 sc, 2 sc BLO, 3-spike Star-st, 2 sc BLO, 1 sc; rep from * to last 7 sts, ch 6, sk 6 sts, 1 sc. Turn.

Row 8: Ch 1, 1 sc, *ch 6, sk ch6-sp, 3 sc BLO, 2 hdc in top of Star-st, 3 sc BLO; rep from * to last ch6-sp, ch 6, sk ch6-sp, 1 sc. Turn.

Row 9: Ch 1, 1 sc BLO, *6 sc BLO in unworked sts 3 rows below (work behind ch6-sp), 8 sc BLO; rep from * to last ch6-sp, 6 sc BLO in unworked sts 3 rows below (work behind ch6-sp), 1 sc. Turn.

Row 10: Rep Row 2.

Rep Rows 3–10 for pattern.

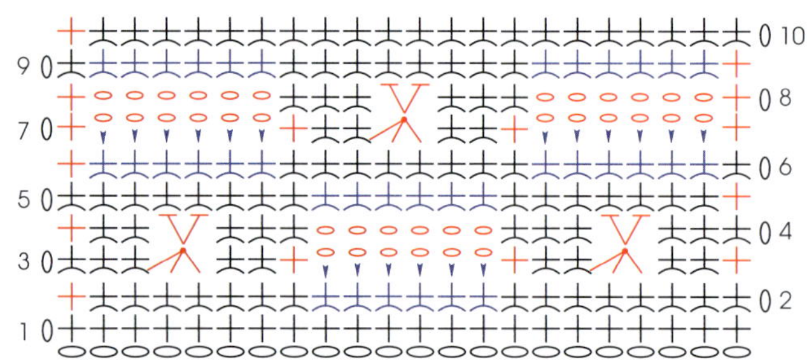

CUMULUS RIDGE STITCH

4-spike star stitches are framed by back loop single crochet to create soft, cloud like shapes that add depth and texture.

Note: *this pattern is worked over a multiple of 8 sts plus 6. Starting chains do not count as sts throughout.*

Start: Chain a multiple of 8 plus 7.

Row 1 (WS): 1 sc in back ridge (bump) of second ch from hook, 1 sc in back ridge (bump) of each ch to end. Turn.

Row 2: Ch 1, 1 sc BLO in each st to last st, 1 sc. Turn.

Row 3: Ch 1, 1 sc, *1 sc BLO, 4-spike Star-st, 1 sc BLO in st just worked, ch 4, sk 4 sts; rep from * to last 5 sts, 1 sc BLO, 4-spike Star-st, 1 sc BLO in st just worked, 1 sc. Turn.

Row 4: Ch 1,1 sc, 4 hdc in top of next Star-st, *ch 4, 5 hdc in top of next Star-st; rep from * to last st, 1 sc. Turn.

Row 5: Ch 1, 4 sc BLO, 2 sc BLO in next st, (sk 1 st, 2 sc BLO, sk 1 st) in unworked sts 3 rows below (work behind ch4-sp), *2 sc BLO in next st, 2 sc BLO, 2 sc BLO in next st, (sk 1 st, 2 sc BLO, sk 1 st) in unworked sts 3 rows below (work behind ch4-sp); rep from * to last 5 sts, 2 sc BLO in next st, 3 sc BLO, 1 sc. Turn.

Row 6: Rep Row 2.

Row 7: Ch 1, 1 sc, *ch 4, sk 4 sts, 1 sc BLO, 4-spike Star-st, 1 sc BLO in st just worked; rep from * to last 5 sts, ch 4, sk 4 sts, 1 sc. Turn.

Row 8: Ch 1,1 sc, ch 4, *5 hdc in top of next Star-st, ch 4; rep from * to last st, 1 sc. Turn.

Row 9: Ch 1, 2 sc BLO in first st, (sk 1 st, 2 sc BLO, sk 1 st) in unworked sts 3 rows below (work behind ch4-sp), *2 sc BLO in next st, 2 sc BLO, 2 sc BLO in next st, (sk 1 st, 2 sc BLO, sk 1 st) in unworked sts 3 rows below (work behind ch4-sp); rep to last st, 2 sc in last st. Turn.

Row 10: Rep Row 2.

Rep Rows 3–10 for pattern.

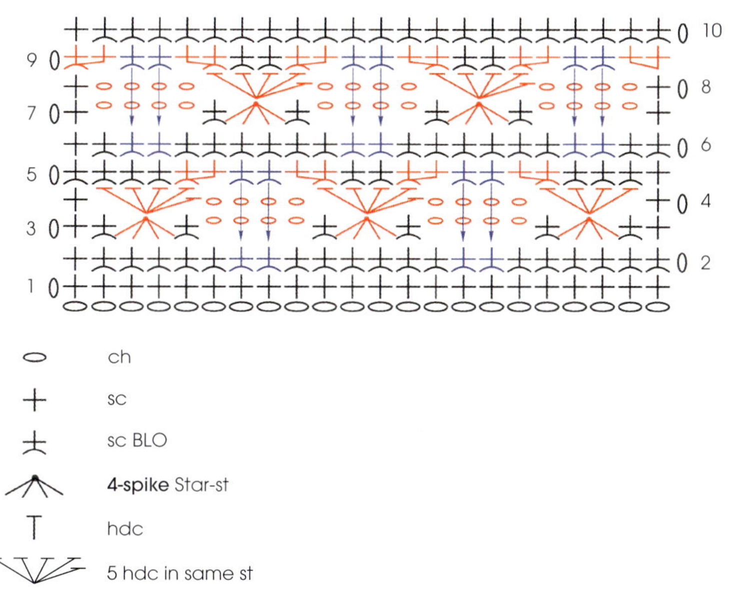

DRAGON-SCALE RIDGE STITCH

Single crochet ribbing worked in combination with half double, double, half treble and treble crochet stitches create a flowing but structured fabric that resembles smooth scales.

Note: *this pattern is worked over a multiple of 14 sts plus 10. Starting chains do not count as sts throughout.*

Start: Chain a multiple of 14 plus 11.

Row 1 (WS): 1 sc in back ridge (bump) of second ch from hook, 1 sc in back ridge (bump) of each ch to end. Turn.

Row 2: Ch 1, 1 sc BLO in each st to last st, 1 sc. Turn.

Row 3: Ch 1, 9 sc BLO, 1 sc, ch 4, sk 4 sts, *1 sc, 8 sc BLO, 1 sc, ch 4, sk 4 sts; rep from * to last 10 sts, 1 sc, 8 sc BLO, 1 sc. Turn.

Row 4: Ch 1, 1 sc, 1 hdc, 1 dc, 1 htr, 2 tr, 1 htr, 1 dc, 1 hdc, 1 sc, *ch 4, sk ch4-sp, 1 sc, 1 hdc, 1 dc, 1 htr, 2 tr, 1 htr, 1 dc, 1 hdc, 1 sc; rep from * to end. Turn.

Row 5: Ch 1, 10 sc BLO, 4 sc BLO in unworked sts 3 rows below (work behind ch4-sp), *10 sc BLO, 6 sc BLO in unworked sts 3 rows below (work behind ch6-sp); rep from * to last 10 sts, 9 sc BLO, 1 sc. Turn.

Row 6: Rep Row 2.

Row 7: Ch 1, 2 sc BLO, 1 sc, ch 4, sk 4 sts, *1 sc, 8 sc BLO, 1 sc, ch 4, sk 4 sts; rep from * to last 3 sts, 1 sc, 1 sc BLO, 1 sc. Turn.

Row 8: Ch 3, 1 dc, 1 hdc, 1 sc, ch 4, sk ch4-sp, *1 sc, 1 hdc, 1 dc, 1 htr, 2 tr, 1 htr, 1 dc, 1 hdc, 1 sc, ch 4, sk ch4-sp; rep from * to last 3 sts, 1 sc, 1 hdc, 1 dc. Turn.

Row 9: Ch 1, 3 sc BLO, 4 sc BLO in unworked sts 3 rows below (work behind ch4-sp), *10 sc BLO, 4 sc BLO in unworked sts 3 rows below (work behind ch4-sp); rep from * to last 3 sts, 2 sc BLO, 1 sc. Turn.

Rows 10: Rep Row 2.

Rep Rows 3–10 for pattern.

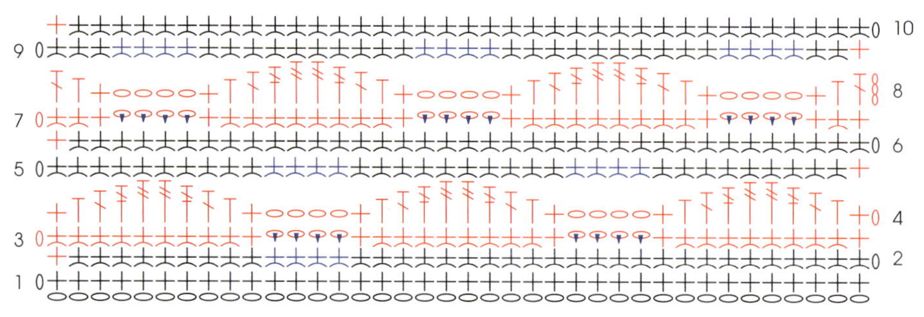

TEXTURE, LACE, AND COLORWORK

DRAGON'S EYE RIDGE STITCH

Larger oval motifs are framed by double rows of single-crochet ribbing, creating a feeling of flow and movement.

Note: *this pattern is worked over a multiple of 16 sts plus 10. Starting chains do not count as sts throughout.*

Start: Chain a multiple of 16 plus 11.

Row 1 (WS): 1 sc in back ridge (bump) of second ch from hook, 1 sc in back ridge (bump) of each ch to end. Turn.

Row 2: Ch 1, 1 sc BLO in each st to last st, 1 sc. Turn.

Row 3: Ch 1, *1 sc, 1 hdc, 1 dc, 1 htr, 2 tr, 1 htr, 1 dc, 1 hdc, 1 sc, ch 6, sk 6 sts; rep from * to last 10 sts, 1 sc, 1 hdc, 1 dc, 1 htr, 2 tr, 1 htr, 1 dc, 1 hdc, 1 sc. Turn.

Row 4: Ch 1, *1 sc, 1 hdc, 1 dc, 1 htr, 2 tr, 1 htr, 1 dc, 1 hdc, 1 sc, ch 6, sk ch6-sp; rep from * to last 10 sts, 1 sc, 1 hdc, 1 dc, 1 htr, 2 tr, 1 htr, 1 dc, 1 hdc, 1 sc. Turn.

Row 5: Ch 1, *10 sc BLO, 6 sc BLO in unworked sts 3 rows below (work behind ch6-sp); rep from * to last 10 sts, 9 sc BLO, 1 sc. Turn.

Rows 6–8: Rep Row 2.

Row 9: Ch 1, 2 sc, ch 6, sk 6 sts, *1 sc, 1 hdc, 1 dc, 1 htr, 2 tr, 1 htr, 1 dc, 1 hdc, 1 sc, ch 6, sk 6 sts; rep from * to last 2 sts, 2 sc. Turn.

Row 10: Ch 1, 1 sc, 1 sc BLO, ch 6, sk ch6-sp, *1 sc, 1 hdc, 1 dc, 1 htr, 2 tr, 1 htr, 1 dc, 1 hdc, 1 sc, ch 6, sk ch6-sp; rep from * to last 2 sts, 1 sc BLO, 1 sc. Turn.

Row 11: Ch 1, 2 sc BLO, 6 sc BLO in unworked sts 3 rows below (work behind ch6-sp), *10 sc BLO, 6 sc BLO in unworked sts 3 rows below (work behind ch6-sps); rep from * to last 2 sts, 1 sc BLO, 1 sc. Turn.

Rows 12–13: Rep Row 2.

Rep Rows 3–13 for pattern.

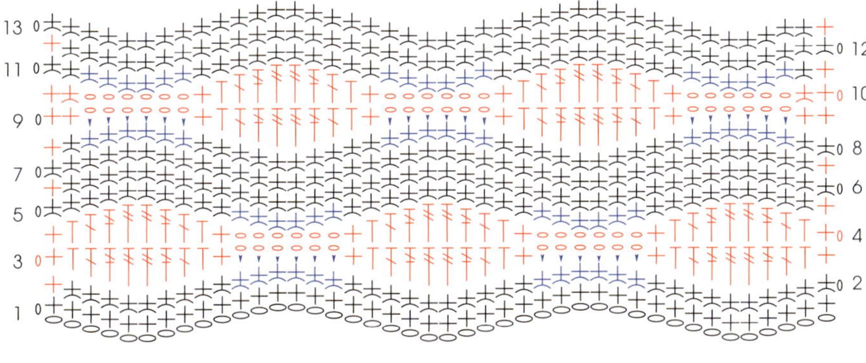

- ch
- sc
- sc BLO
- hdc
- dc
- htr
- tr

COLORWORK PROJECT

Drop by Drop Shawl

The Drop by Drop shawl is worked from the center of the top down, making it easily adjustable. The simple ribbing ridges outline each diamond without interruption, creating a smooth, continuous flow across the width of the fabric.

This shawl uses three colors for a striking effect, but it would be equally dramatic in two or even one color, which would emphasize its textured design. The stitch pattern invites endless creative colorwork possibilities, making each version of Drop by Drop truly unique.

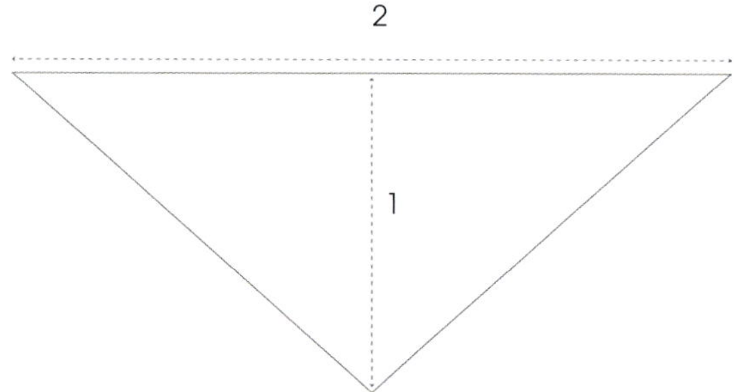

YOU WILL NEED

YARN

Malabrigo Sock (100% superwash Merino wool), 3-ply/light fingering, 100g (402m/440yds), in the following shades:

Main color (MC): Gingy (SW358), 1 skein

Contrast color 1 (CC1): Under the Sea (SW362), 1 skein

Contrast color 2 (CC2): Cian (SW683), 1 skein

HOOKS

Size 3.5mm (US E/4) hook

TENSION

22 sts and 20 rows measure 10 x 10cm (4 x 4in) over Rib st pattern using a 3.5mm (US E/4) hook.

MEASUREMENTS

Depth (1): 60cm (24in)

Wingspan (2): 135cm (54in)

ABBREVIATIONS

BLO	back loop only
CC	contrast color
ch	chain
ch-sp	chain space
dc	double crochet
hdc	half double crochet
htr	half treble crochet
M	marker
MC	main color
PM	place marker
rep	repeat
RS	right side of work
sc	single crochet
sk	skip/miss
st(s)	stitch(es)
tr	treble crochet
WS	wrong side of work

SPECIAL STITCHES

Extended single crochet (esc) (see Chapter 1: special stitches)

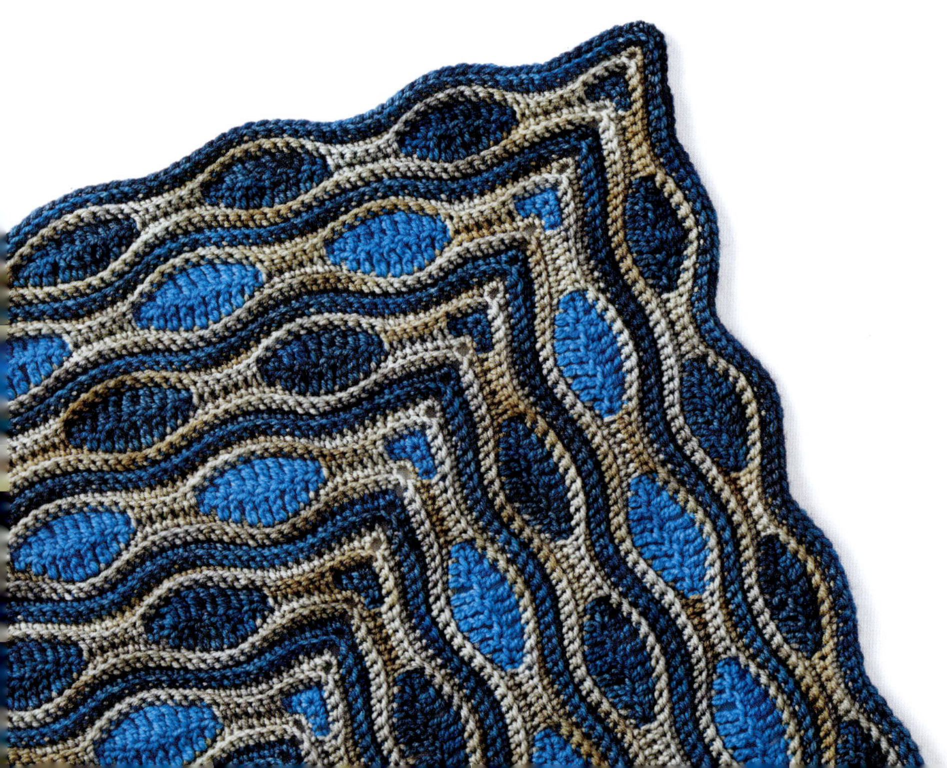

INSTRUCTIONS

Using MC, make a magic ring.

Row 1 (WS): Ch 1, 5 sc into ring. Turn. (5 sts)

Row 2 (RS): Ch 1, 2 sc BLO in first st, 1 sc BLO, 3 sc BLO in next st, 1 sc BLO, 2 sc in last st. Turn. (9 sts)

Row 3: Ch 1, 2 sc BLO in first st, 3 sc BLO, 3 sc BLO in next st, PM in second of these 3 sts to mark center st, 3 sc BLO, 2 sc in last st. Turn. (13 sts)

Note: *move the marker to the central stitch of each row as you work.*

Row 4: Ch 1, 2 sc BLO in first st, 1 sc BLO in each st to marked st, 3 sc BLO in marked st, 1 sc BLO in each st to last st, 2 sc in last st. Turn. (4 sts increased)

Rows 5–8: Rep Row 4. (33 sts)

Change to CC1.

Rows 9 and 10: Rep Row 4. (41 sts)

Change to MC.

Rows 11 and 12: Rep Row 4. (49 sts)

Change to CC1.

Row 13: Ch 1, 2 sc in first st, ch 6, sk 6 sts, 1 sc, 1 hdc, 1 dc, 1 htr, 2 tr, 1 htr, 1 dc, 1 hdc,1 sc, ch 6, sk 6 sts, 1 sc, 3 sc in marked st, 1 sc, ch 6, sk 6 sts, 1 sc, 1 hdc, 1 dc, 1 htr, 2 tr, 1 htr, 1 dc, 1 hdc, 1 sc, ch 6, sk 6 sts, 2 sc in last st. Turn. (29 sts, 4 ch-sps)

Row 14: Ch 1, 2 sc in first st, 1 sc, ch 6, sk ch6-sp, 1 sc, 1 hdc, 1 dc, 1 htr, 2 tr, 1 htr, 1 dc, 1 hdc, 1 sc, ch 6, sk ch6-sp, 2 sc, 3 sc in marked st, 2 sc, ch 6, sk ch6-sp, 1 sc, 1 hdc, 1 dc, 1 htr, 2 tr, 1 htr, 1 dc, 1 hdc, 1 sc, ch 6, skip ch6-sp, 1 sc, 2 sc in last st. Turn. (33 sts, 4 ch-sps)

Note: *when working into skipped sts 3 rows below, always work behind the chains.*

Change to MC.

Row 15: Ch 1, 2 sc BLO in first st, 2 sc BLO, 6 sc BLO in each skipped st 3 rows below (work behind the ch-sps), 10 sc BLO, 6 sc BLO in each skipped st 3 rows below, 3 sc BLO, 3 sc BLO in marked st, 3 sc BLO, 6 sc BLO in each skipped st 3 rows below, 10 sc BLO, 6 sc BLO in each skipped st 3 rows below, 2 sc BLO, 2 sc in last st. Turn. (61 sts)

Row 16: Rep Row 4. (65 sts)

Change to CC1.

Rows 17 and 18: Rep Row 4. (73 sts)

Change to MC.

Rows 19 and 20: Rep Row 4. (81 sts)

Change to CC2.

Row 21: Ch 1, 2 sc in first st, ch 6, sk 6 sts, *1 sc, 1 hdc, 1 dc, 1 htr, 2 tr, 1 htr, 1 dc, 1 hdc, 1 sc, ch 6, sk 6 sts; rep from * to 1 st before marked st, 1 sc, 3 sc in marked st, 1 sc, ch 6, sk 6 sts, rep from * to last st, 2 sc in last st. Turn. (49 sts, 6 ch-sps)

Row 22: Ch 1, 2 sc in first st, 1 sc, *ch 6, sk ch6-sp, 1 sc, 1 hdc, 1 dc, 1 htr, 2 tr, 1 htr, 1 dc, 1 hdc, 1 sc; rep from * to last ch6-sp before marked st, ch 6, sk ch6-sp, 2 sc, 3 sc in marked st, 2 sc, rep from * to last ch6-sp, ch 6, sk ch6-sp, 1 sc, 2 sc in last st. Turn. (53 sts, 6 ch-sps)

Cut CC2 and continue with MC.

Row 23: Ch 1, 2 sc BLO in first st, 2 sc BLO, *6 sc BLO in each skipped st 3 rows below, 10 sc BLO; rep from * to last ch6-sp before marked st, 6 sc BLO in skipped sts 3 rows below, 3 sc BLO, 3 sc BLO in marked st, 3 sc BLO, rep from * to last ch6-sp, 6 sc BLO in skipped sts 3 rows below, 2 sc BLO, 2 sc in last st. Turn. (93 sts)

Row 24: Rep Row 4. (97 sts)

Change to CC1.

Rows 25 and 26: Rep Row 4. (105 sts)

Rows 27–90: Repeat Rows 11–26 another 4 times, maintaining the color changes as set and continuing to increase by 4 sts each row (a total of 64 sts per repeat). (361 sts)

Rows 91–98: Repeat Rows 11–18 once more, finishing on a CC1 row. (393 sts)

Fasten off yarn and weave in ends.

FINISHING

Wet block your shawl to the finished measurements. Once damp, lay it out on a flat surface. Make sure all edges are straight, to set the triangular shape. Align the rows so the waves are evenly spaced, and stretch the corner diamonds to make them taller and fuller.

CHART INSTRUCTIONS

Start with MC. Alternate colors every 2 rows.

Rows 1–8: Using MC, work Chart Rows 1–8.

Rows 9–10: Using CC1, work Chart Rows 9–10.

Rows 11–12: Using MC, work Chart Rows 11–12.

Rows 13–14 (diamonds): Using CC1, work Chart Rows 13–14.

Rows 15–20: Starting with MC, work Chart Rows 15–20, alternating with CC1 every 2 rows.

Rows 21–22 (diamonds): Using CC2, work Chart Rows 21–22.

Rows 23–24: Using MC, work Chart Rows 23–24.

Rows 25-26: Using CC, work Chart Rows 3 and 4.

Rows 27–90: Rep Rows 11–26 another 4 times.

Rows 91–98: Rep Rows 11–18 once more. (393 sts)

FINISHING

See written instructions.

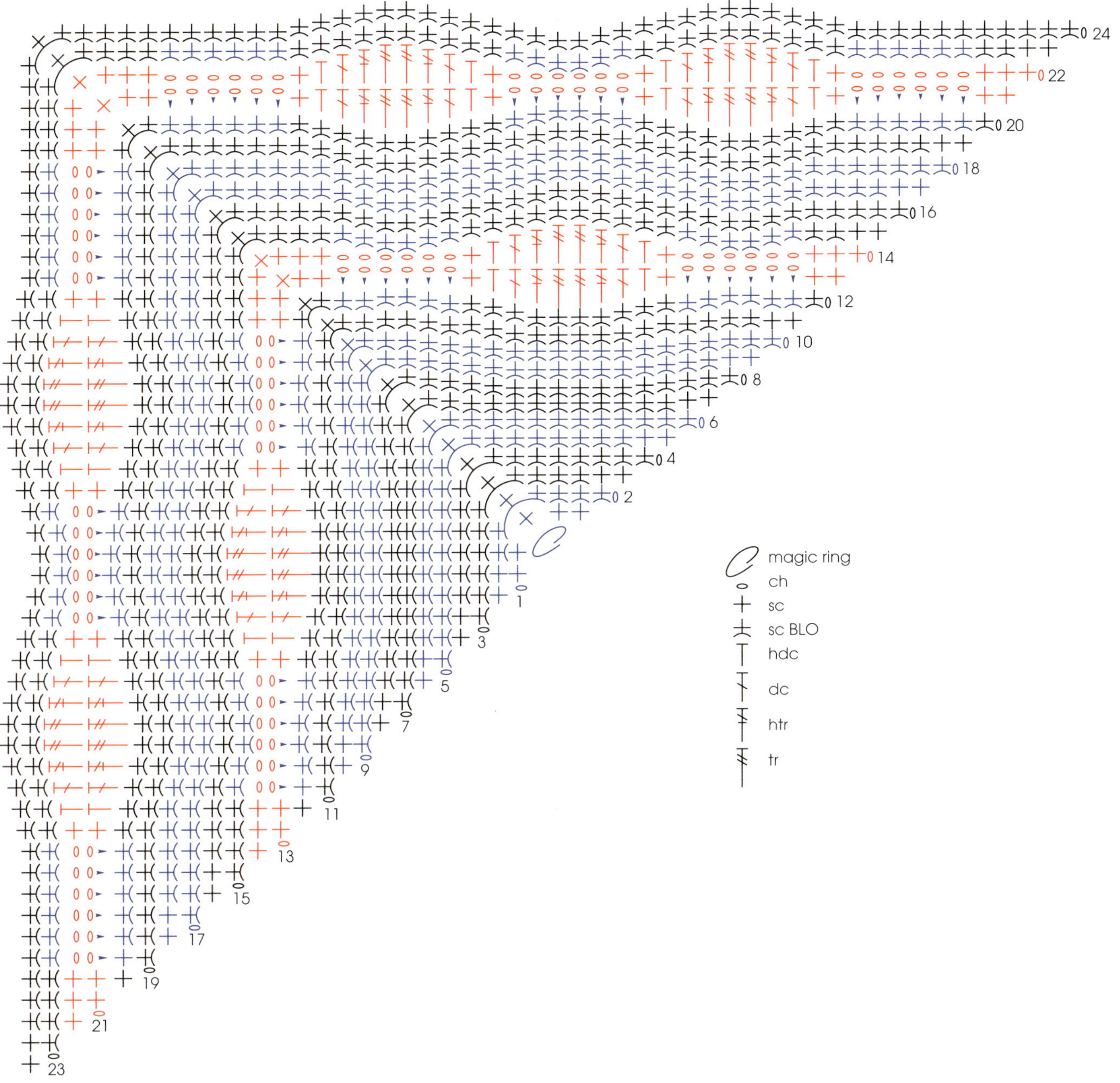
magic ring
ch
sc
sc BLO
hdc
dc
htr
tr
1
2
3
4
5
6
7
8
9
10
11
12
13
14
15
16
17
18
19
20
21
22
23
24

CHAPTER 4:

SINGLE-CROCHET RIBBING VARIATIONS

The stitch patterns in this chapter use linen stitch as a foundation, and are inspired by the intricate patterns found in tree bark and leaves. You will use the extended single crochet stitch to replace some of the single crochet stitches, creating delicate lines, bold ribbing, and intricate honeycomb patterns.

The stitch patterns are introduced gradually, from the simplest to the most complex, allowing you to practice different ways of working the extended single crochet stitch: vertically, diagonally, and in pairs.

STITCH FOCUS:

Extended single crochet two rows below

NOTES ON TECHNIQUE

Extended single crochet (esc) stitches are always worked on RS rows and in stitches two rows below. Depending on their placement, esc stitches can be vertical or angled diagonally to the left or right.

You will work the esc in front of the chain space from the previous row, through the legs of the sc or the top V of the esc beneath it. If you find it difficult to work the esc stitches around the legs of the first row of single crochet, you can work the esc into the loops of the sc instead. This will not affect the look of the stitch pattern.

The ch-sp above the stitch you have just worked should be skipped, as it would be if you had worked into it on a regular linen stitch pattern. For example, if the pattern says: (esc, ch 1, 1 sc), work it as follows: esc into the stitch below the ch-sp, leave the ch-sp itself unworked, ch 1, 1 sc in the next ch-sp.

SPECIAL STITCHES

Extended sc (esc): Working in front of ch-sp, insert hook in indicated space: through the sc legs (A) or a top V of esc (B), yo, pull up a loop (2 loops on hook) yo, draw hook through 1 loop, yo, draw hook through both loops.

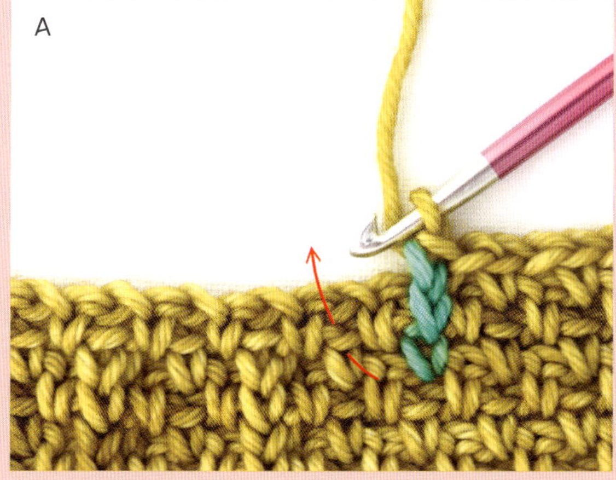

Insert the hook into legs of sc two rows below.

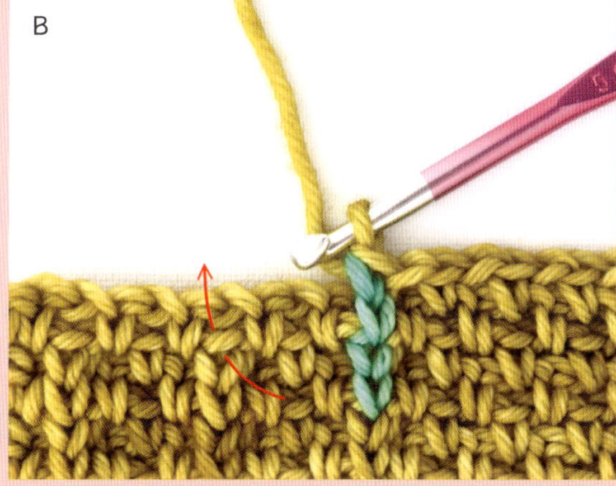

Insert the hook into top V of esc two rows below.

GRASS STITCH

Single crochet stitches and chains are used to create an offset, checkered pattern, which adds subtle depth to the fabric.

Note: *this pattern is worked over a multiple of 4 sts plus 5. Starting chains do not count as sts throughout.*

Start: Chain a multiple of 4 plus 6.

Row 1 (RS): 1 sc in back ridge (bump) of second ch from hook, 1 sc in back ridge (bump) of each ch to end. Turn.

Row 2 (WS): Ch 1, 2 sc, *ch 1, sk 1 st, 1 sc; rep from * to last st, 1 sc. Turn.

Remember *to work esc in front of the ch-sp into the st below (see Chapter 4: Special Stitches).*

Row 3: Ch 1, 1 sc, ch 1, *1 esc, ch 1, 1 sc, ch 1; rep from * to last ch-sp, 1 esc, ch 1, sk 1 st, 1 sc. Turn.

Row 4: Ch 1, 1 sc, *1 sc, ch 1; rep from * to last ch-sp, 1 sc in last ch-sp, 1 sc in last st. Turn.

Row 5: Ch 1, 1 sc, *ch 1, 1 sc, ch 1, 1 esc; rep from * to last ch-sp, ch 1, 1 sc in last ch-sp, ch 1, sk 1 st, 1 sc. Turn.

Row 6: Rep Row 4.

Rep Rows 3–6 for pattern.

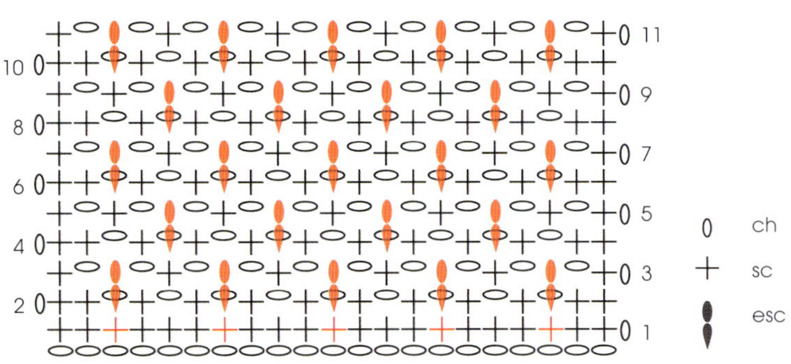

FINE LINEN RIB STITCH

Narrow vertical lines are added to linen stitch using extended single crochet stitches, creating a refined, structured appearance.

Note: *this pattern is worked over a multiple of 4 sts plus 5. Starting chains do not count as sts throughout.*

Start: Chain a multiple of 4 plus 6.

Row 1 (RS): 1 sc in back ridge (bump) of second ch from hook, 1 sc in back ridge (bump) of each ch to end. Turn.

Row 2 (WS): Ch 1, 2 sc, *ch 1, sk 1 st, 1 sc; rep from * to last st, 1 sc. Turn.

Remember *to work esc in front of the ch-sp into the st below (see Chapter 4: Special Stitches).*

Row 3: Ch 1, 1 sc, ch 1, *1 esc, ch 1, 1 sc, ch 1; rep from * to last ch-sp, 1 esc, ch 1, sk 1 st, 1 sc in last st. Turn.

Row 4: Ch 1, 1 sc, *1 sc, ch 1; rep from * to last ch-sp, 1 sc in last ch-sp, 1 sc in last st. Turn.

Rep Rows 3–4 for pattern.

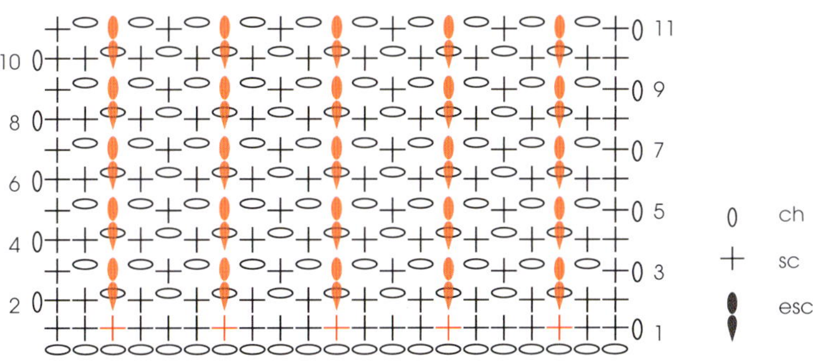

FLOWING LINEN RIB STITCH

The ribs in this pattern form gentle waves by placing extended single crochet stitches diagonally, creating a softly flowing effect.

Note: *this pattern is worked over a multiple of 4 sts plus 5. Starting chains do not count as sts throughout.*

Start: Chain a multiple of 4 plus 6.

Row 1 (RS): 1 sc in back ridge (bump) of second ch from hook, 1 sc in back ridge (bump) of each ch to end. Turn.

Row 2 (WS): Ch 1, 2 sc, *ch 1, sk 1 st, 1 sc; rep from * to last st, 1 sc. Turn.

Row 3: Ch 1, 1 sc, ch 1, 1 sc, *ch 1, 1 esc under same ch-sp, ch 1, sk 1 ch-sp, 1 sc; rep from * to last 2 sts, ch 1, sk 1 st, 1 sc. Turn.

Row 4 and all following WS rows: Ch 1, 1 sc, *1 sc, ch 1; rep from * to last ch-sp, 1 sc in last ch-sp, 1 sc in last st. Turn.

Note: *from Row 5, work all esc into the top V of the esc below (see Chapter 4: Special Stitches).*

Row 5: Ch 1, 1 sc, (ch 1, 1 sc) twice, *ch 1, 1 esc, ch 1, 1 sc; rep from * to last ch-sp, ch 1, 1 esc, ch 1, sk 1 st, 1 sc in last st. Turn.

Row 7: Rep Row 5.

Row 9: Ch 1, 1 sc, ch 1, 1 sc, *ch 1, 1 esc, ch 1, 1 sc; rep from * to last 2 sts, ch 1, sk 1 st, 1 sc. Turn.

Row 11: Ch 1, 1 sc, *ch 1, 1 esc, ch 1, 1 sc; rep from * to last ch-sp, ch 1, 1 sc in last ch-sp, ch 1, sk 1 st, 1 sc in last st. Turn.

Row 13: Rep Row 11.

Row 15: Rep Row 9.

Row 16: Rep Row 4.

Rep Rows 5–16 for pattern.

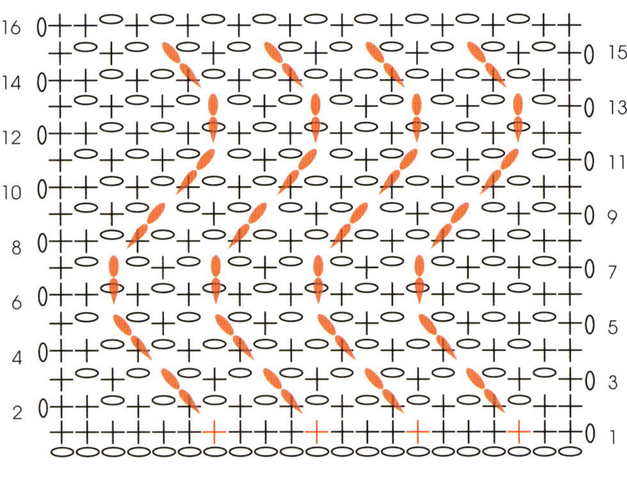

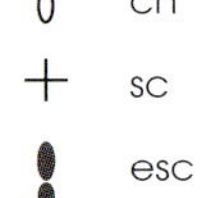

BOLD LINEN RIB STITCH

Bold, wide ribbing is formed using two extended single crochet stitches. Added depth is achieved by working a ch-1 over these two stitches on the wrong side rows, sharply defining the ribs.

Note: *this pattern is worked over a multiple of 4 sts plus 5. Starting chains do not count as sts throughout.*

Start: Chain a multiple of 4 plus 6.

Row 1 (RS): 1 sc in back ridge (bump) of second ch from hook, 1 sc in back ridge (bump) of each ch to end. Turn.

Row 2: Ch 1, 2 sc, *ch 1, sk 1 st, 1 sc; rep from * to last st, 1 sc. Turn.

Remember *to work esc in front of the ch-sp into the st below (see Chapter 4: Special Stitches).*

Row 3: Ch 1, 1 sc, ch 1, *2 esc in st under next ch-sp, ch 1, 1 sc, ch 1; rep from * to last ch-sp, 2 esc in st under last ch-sp, ch 1, sk 1 st, 1 sc in last st. Turn.

Row 4: Ch 1, 1 sc, *1 sc, ch 1; rep from * to last ch-sp, 1 sc in last ch-sp, 1 sc in last st. Turn.

Row 5: Ch 1, 1 sc, ch 1, *2 esc, ch 1, 1 sc, ch 1; rep from * to last ch-sp, 2 esc, ch 1, sk 1 st, 1 sc in last st. Turn.

Rep Rows 4 and 5 for pattern.

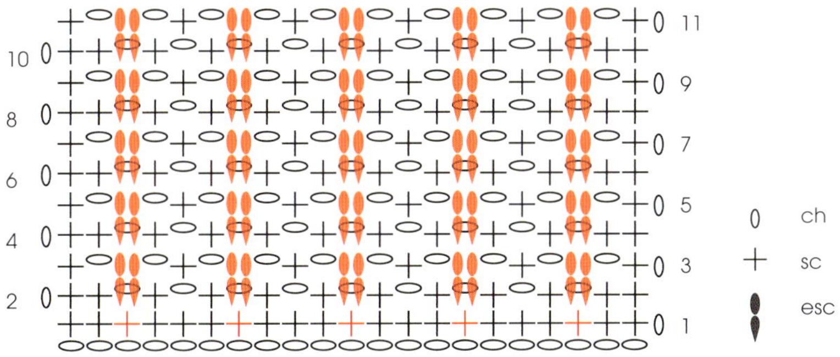

PETITE HONEYCOMB STITCH

Alternating diagonal extended single crochet stitches create a rich honeycomb texture.

Note: *this pattern is worked over a multiple of 4 sts plus 1. Starting chains do not count as sts throughout.*

Start: Chain a multiple of 4 plus 2.

Row 1 (RS): 1 sc in back ridge (bump) of second ch from hook, 1 sc in back ridge (bump) of each ch to end. Turn.

Row 2 (WS): Ch 1, 2 sc, *ch 1, sk 1 st, 1 sc; rep from * to last st, 1 sc. Turn.

Row 3: Ch 1, 1 sc, ch 1, *sk 1 ch-sp, 1 esc under next ch-sp, ch 1, 1 sc in same ch-sp, ch 1, 1 esc in same st as last esc; rep from * to last 2 sts, ch 1, sk 1 st, 1 sc. Turn.

Row 4: Ch 1, 1 sc, *1 sc, ch 1; rep from * to last ch-sp, 1 sc in last ch-sp, 1 sc in last st. Turn.

Note: *from Row 5, work all esc into the top V of the esc below (see Chapter 4: Special Stitches).*

Row 5: Ch 1, 1 sc, ch 1, 1 sc, ch 1, *2 esc, ch 1, 1 sc, ch 1; rep from * to last 2 sts, sk 1 st, 1 sc. Turn.

Row 6: Rep Row 4.

Row 7: Ch 1, 1 sc, ch 1, *1 esc, ch 1, 1 sc, ch 1, 1 esc; rep from * to last 2 sts, ch 1, sk 1 st, 1 sc. Turn.

Row 8: Rep Row 4.

Rep Rows 5–8 for pattern.

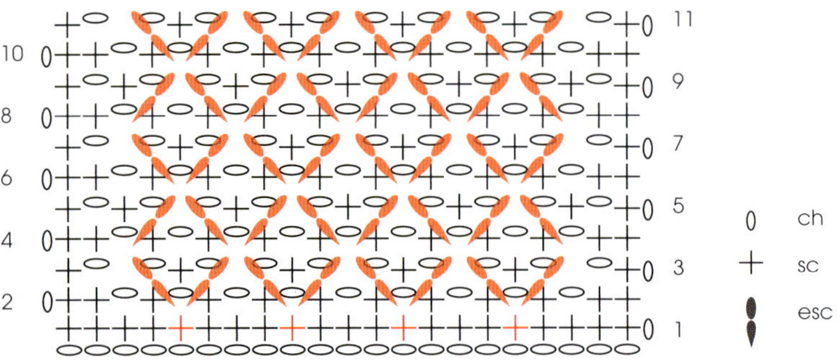

LANTERN STITCH

A variation on Petite Honeycomb Stitch, which uses an extra row of vertical extended single crochet stitches to create space within each element.

Note: *this pattern is worked over a multiple of 4 sts plus 1. Starting chains do not count as sts throughout.*

Start: Chain a multiple of 4 plus 2.

Row 1 (RS): 1 sc in back ridge (bump) of second ch from hook, 1 sc in back ridge (bump) of each ch to end. Turn.

Row 2 (WS): Ch 1, 2 sc, *ch 1, sk 1 st, 1 sc; rep from * to last st, 1 sc. Turn.

Row 3: Ch 1, 1 sc, ch 1, *sk 1 ch-sp and 1 st, 1 esc, ch 1, 1 sc in ch-sp above esc just worked, ch 1, 1 esc in same st as last esc; rep from * to last ch-sp, ch 1, 1 sc in last st. Turn.

Row 4 and all following WS rows: Ch 1, 1 sc, *1 sc, ch 1; rep from * to last ch-sp, 1 sc in last ch-sp, 1 sc in last st. Turn.

Work *all esc into the top V of the esc below (see Chapter 4: Special Stitches).*

Row 5: Ch 1, 1 sc, ch 1, 1 esc, ch 1, 1 sc, ch 1, *2 esc, ch 1, 1 sc, ch 1; rep from * to last esc, 1 esc, ch 1, sk 1 st, 1 sc in last st. Turn.

Row 7: Ch 1, 1 sc, ch 1, 1 sc, ch 1, *2 esc, ch 1, 1 sc, ch 1; rep from * to last 2 sts, sk 1 st, 1 sc. Turn.

Row 9: Rep Row 7.

Row 11: Rep Row 5.

Row 12: Rep Row 4.

Rep Rows 5–12 for pattern.

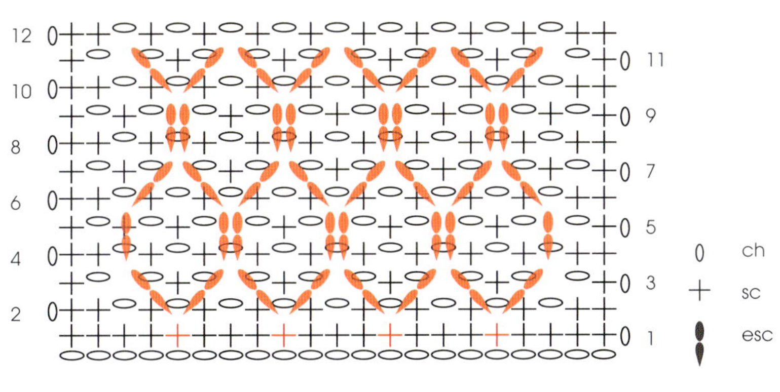

EXTENDED LANTERN STITCH

Double extended single-crochet ribbing combines with honeycomb details to create a texture that resembles strings of tiny lights.

Note: *this pattern is worked over a multiple of 8 sts plus 5. Starting chains do not count as sts throughout.*

Start: Chain a multiple of 8 plus 6.

Row 1 (RS): 1 sc in back ridge (bump) of second ch from hook, 1 sc in back ridge (bump) of each ch to end. Turn.

Row 2 (WS): Ch 1, 2 sc, *ch 1, sk 1 st, 1 sc; rep from * to last st, 1 sc. Turn.

Row 3: Ch 1, 1 sc, ch 1, *sk 1 ch-sp and 1 st, 1 esc, ch 1, 1 sc in ch-sp above esc just worked, ch 1, 1 esc in same st as last esc; rep from * to last ch-sp, ch 1, 1 sc in last st. Turn.

Row 4: Ch 1, 1 sc, *1 sc, ch 1; rep from * to last ch-sp, 1 sc in last ch-sp, 1 sc in last st. Turn.

Work *all esc into the top V of the esc below (see Chapter 4: Special Stitches).*

Row 5: Ch 1, 1 sc, ch 1, 1 sc, *ch 1, 2 esc, ch 1, 1 sc; rep from * to last 2 sts, ch 1, sk 1 st, 1 sc. Turn.

Row 6: Rep Row 4.

Rows 7–10: Rep Rows 5 and 6 twice more.

Row 11: Ch 1, 1 sc, ch 1, *1 esc, ch 1, 1 sc, ch 1, 1 esc; rep from * to last 2 sts, ch 1, sk 1 st, 1 sc. Turn.

Row 12: Rep Row 4.

Rep Rows 5–12 for pattern.

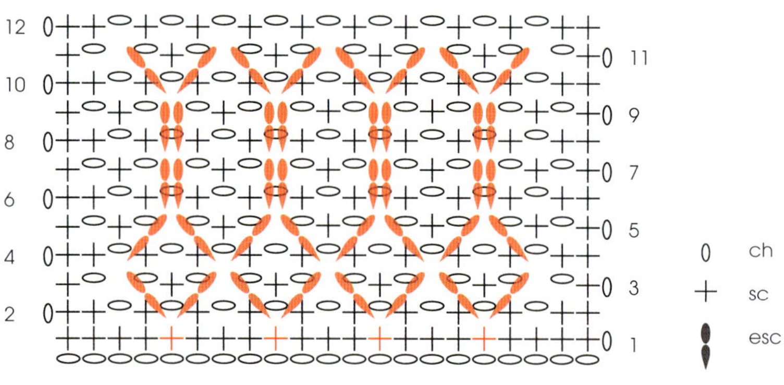

RIBBED LANTERN STITCH

Diagonal extended single crochets are paired with bold simple ribbing to create a linear pattern of diamond motifs.

Note: *this pattern is worked over a multiple of 8 sts plus 5. Starting chains do not count as sts throughout.*

Start: Chain a multiple of 8 plus 6.

Row 1 (RS): 1 sc in back ridge (bump) of second ch from hook, 1 sc in back ridge (bump) of each ch to end. Turn.

Row 2 (WS): Ch 1, 2 sc, *ch 1, sk 1 st, 1 sc; rep from * to last st, 1 sc. Turn.

Row 3: Ch 1, 1 sc, *ch 1, 2 esc in sc under next ch-sp, ch 1, 1 sc; rep from * to end, working last sc on final repeat into last st of row instead of ch-sp. Turn.

Row 4: Ch 1, 1 sc, *1 sc, ch 1; rep from * to last ch-sp, 1 sc in last ch-sp, 1 sc in last st. Turn.

Work *all esc into the top V of the esc below (see Chapter 4: Special Stitches).*

Row 5: Ch 1, 1 sc, ch 1, 2 esc, *ch 1, 1 esc, ch 1, 1 sc, ch 1, 1 esc, ch 1, 2 esc; rep from * to last 2 sts, ch 1, sk 1 st, 1 sc. Turn.

Row 6: Rep Row 4.

Rows 7 and 8: Rep Rows 5 and 6.

Row 9: Ch 1, 1 sc, ch 1, 2 esc, *ch 1, 1 sc, ch 1, 2 esc; rep from * to last 2 sts, ch 1, sk 1 st, 1 sc. Turn.

Row 10: Rep Row 4.

Rows 11 and 12: Rep Rows 9 and 10.

Rep Rows 5–12 for pattern.

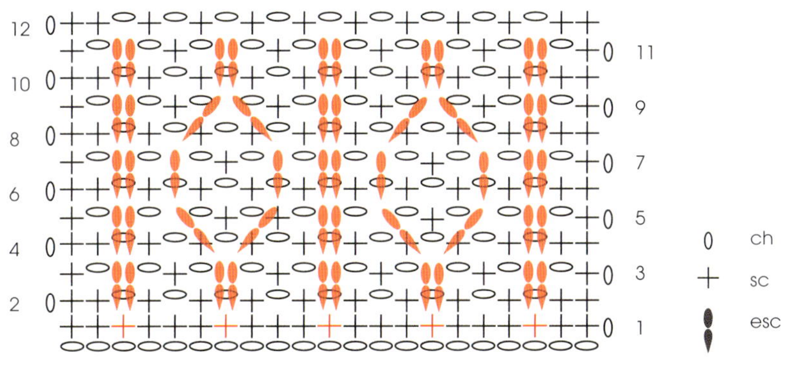

RAISED DIAMOND STITCH

Large diamond shapes are created with extended single crochet lines for a soft but geometric look.

Note: *this pattern is worked over a multiple of 8 sts plus 5. Starting chains do not count as sts throughout.*

Start: Chain a multiple of 8 plus 6.

Row 1 (RS): 1 sc in back ridge (bump) of second ch from hook, 1 sc in back ridge (bump) of each ch to end. Turn.

Row 2 (WS): Ch 1, 2 sc, *ch 1, sk 1 st, 1 sc; rep from * to last st, 1 sc. Turn.

Note: *work all esc into the top V of the esc below (see Chapter 4: Special Stitches).*

Row 3: Ch 1, 1 sc, ch 1, 1 esc, (ch 1, 1 sc) 3 times, *ch 1, 2 esc in sc under next ch-sp, (ch 1, 1 sc) 3 times; rep from * to last ch-sp, ch 1, 1 esc in sc under next ch-sp, ch 1, sk 1 st, 1 sc. Turn.

Row 4 and all following WS rows: Ch 1, 1 sc, *1 sc, ch 1; rep from * to last ch-sp, 1 sc in last ch-sp, 1 sc in last st. Turn.

Row 5: Ch 1, 1 sc, ch 1, 1 sc, *ch 1, 1 esc, ch 1, 1 sc; rep from * to last 2 sts, ch 1, sk 1 st, 1 sc. Turn.

Row 7: Ch 1, 1 sc, ch 1, 1 sc, *ch 1, 1 sc, ch 1, 2 esc, (ch 1, 1 sc) twice; rep from * to last 2 sts, ch 1, sk 1 st, 1 sc. Turn.

Row 9: Rep Row 7.

Row 11: Rep Row 5.

Row 13: Ch 1, 1 sc, *ch 1, 1 esc, (ch 1, 1 sc) 3 times, ch 1, 1 esc; rep from * to last 2 sts, ch 1, sk 1 st, 1 sc. Turn.

Row 15: Ch 1, 1 sc, ch 1, 1 esc, (ch 1, 1 sc) 3 times, *ch 1, 2 esc, (ch 1, 1 sc) 3 times; rep from * to last ch-sp, ch 1, 1 esc, ch 1, sk 1 st, 1 sc in last st. Turn.

Row 16: Rep Row 4.

Rep Rows 5–16 for pattern.

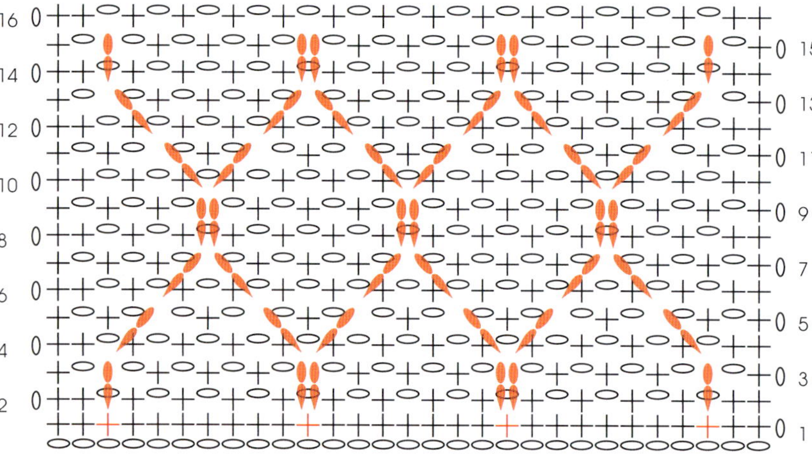

0 ch
+ sc
esc

LOCKING LATTICE STITCH

An intricate design of inerlocking diamonds creates a refined lattice motif, alternating large and small geometric shapes.

Note: *this pattern is worked over a multiple of 8 sts plus 5. Starting chains do not count as sts throughout.*

Start: Chain a multiple of 8 plus 6.

Row 1 (RS): 1 sc in back ridge (bump) of second ch from hook, 1 sc in back ridge (bump) of each ch to end. Turn.

Row 2 (WS): Ch 1, 2 sc, *ch 1, sk 1 st, 1 sc; rep from * to last st, 1 sc. Turn.

Row 3: Ch 1, 1 sc, ch 1, 1 sc,*ch 1, sk 1 st and 1 ch-sp, 1 esc in sc under next ch-sp, ch 1, 1 sc in ch-sp above esc just worked, ch 1, 1 esc in same st as last esc, ch 1, 1 sc; rep from * to last 2 sts, ch 1, sk 1 st, 1 sc. Turn.

Row 4: Ch 1, 1 sc, *1 sc, ch 1; rep from * to last ch-sp, 1 sc in last ch-sp, 1 sc in last st. Turn.

Note: *work all esc into the top V of the esc below (see Chapter 4: Special Stitches).*

Row 5: Ch 1, 1 sc, ch 1, *1 esc, (ch 1, 1 sc) 3 times, ch 1, 1 esc; rep from * to last 2 sts, ch 1, sk 1 st, 1 sc. Turn.

Row 6: Rep Row 4.

Row 7: Ch 1, 1 sc, ch 1, 1 sc, *ch 1, 1 esc, ch 1, 1 sc; rep from * to last 2 sts, sk 1 st, 1 sc. Turn.

Row 8: Rep Row 4.

Rows 9–12: Rep Rows 5–8.

Row 13: Ch 1, 1 sc, ch 1, 1 sc, *ch 1, 1 sc, ch 1, 2 esc, (ch 1, 1 sc) twice; rep from * to last 2 sts, ch 1, sk 1 st, 1 sc. Turn.

Row 14: Rep Row 4.

Rows 15 and 16: Rep Rows 7 and 8.

Rows 17 and 18: Rep Rows 13 and 14.

Rows 19 and 20: Rep Rows 7 and 8.

Rep Rows 5–20 for pattern.

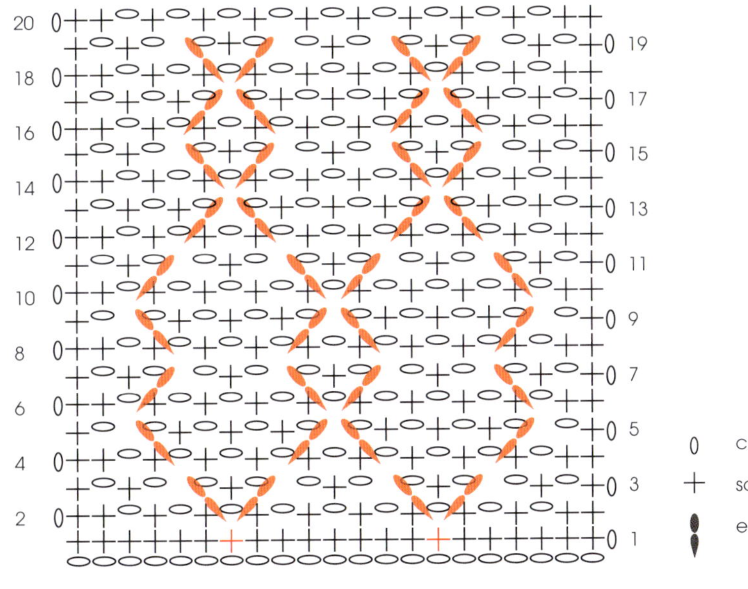

RIB-STITCH PROJECT

Heartstring Shawl

The Heartstring shawl is a celebration of connection and emotion, inspired by the intertwining patterns of roots and vines and the deep ties that pull at the heart.

It starts at one side corner and grows toward the center (bottom corner). The decreases are then worked to shape the shawl to its opposite corner. Its simple, intuitive stitch pattern repeat makes it easy to follow and adjust: continue in the stitch pattern until you reach your desired depth and half the width, then transition to the decreases.

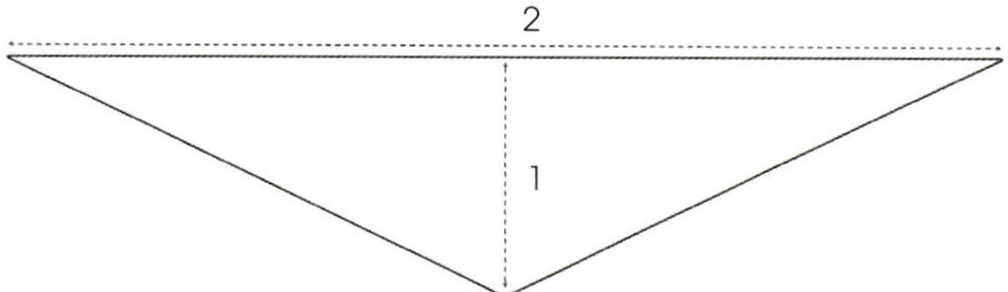

YOU WILL NEED

YARN

Malabrigo Arroyo (100% Merino wool), DK/Sport, 100g (306m/335yds), in the following shade:

Cereza (AR033); 2 skeins

HOOKS

Size 5mm (US H/8) hook

TENSION

26 sts (sc and ch-sp) and 22 rows measure 10 x 10cm (4 x 4in) over linen stitch pattern using a 5mm (US H/8) hook

MEASUREMENTS

Depth (1): 36cm (14¼in)

Wingspan (2): 150cm (59in)

ABBREVIATIONS

BLO	back loop only
CC	contrast color
ch	chain
ch-sp	chain space
dc	double crochet
hdc	half double crochet
htr	half treble crochet
M	marker
MC	main color
PM	place marker
rep	repeat
RS	right side of work
sc	single crochet
sk	skip/miss
sp	space
st(s)	stitch(es)
tr	treble crochet
yo	yarn over
WS	wrong side of work
yo	yarn over

SPECIAL STITCHES

Magic ring (see General Techniques: Basic Stitches)

Bobble stitch (see General Techniques: Special Stitches)

Extended single crochet (esc) (see Chapter 1: Special Stitches and Chapter 4: Special Stitches)

Esc 2 stitches together (esc2tog) (see Chapter 1: Twisted Eyelet Stitch, working into both loops of the st unless otherwise instructed)

INSTRUCTIONS

PATTERN REPEAT

Row 1 (RS): 2 esc, ch 1, 1 sc in next ch-sp, ch 1, 2 esc, ch 1, 1 sc in next ch-sp, sk 1 st, bobble st in next ch-sp, ch 1, 1 sc in next ch-sp, ch 1.

Row 2 (WS): (1 sc in next ch-sp, ch 1) 4 times, ch 1, 1 sc in space between bobble st and next sc, (ch 1, 1 sc in next ch-sp) 3 times, ch 1, sk 2 sts.

Row 3: 2 esc, ch 1, 1 esc in next esc, ch 1, 1 sc in ch-sp above esc just worked, ch 1, 1 esc in next esc, ch 1, 1 sc in next ch-sp, ch 1, 1 esc in next esc, ch 1, 1 sc in ch-sp above esc just worked, ch 1, 1 esc in next esc, ch 1.

Rows 4 and 6: (1 sc in next ch-sp, ch 1) 7 times, 1 sc in next ch-sp.

Row 5: 2 esc, ch 1, (1 esc, ch 1, 1 sc in next ch-sp, ch 1) 3 times, 1 esc, ch 1.

Row 7: 2 esc, ch 1, 1 sc in next ch-sp, ch 1, 1 esc in esc under last ch-sp, 1 esc in next esc, ch 1, 1 sc in ch-sp above esc just worked, (ch 1, 1 sc in next ch-sp) twice, ch 1, 1 esc in esc under last ch-sp, 1 esc in next esc, ch 1, 1 sc in ch-sp above esc just worked, ch 1.

Row 8: Rep Row 4.

BEGINNING AND SET-UP

Note: *starting ch1 does not count as a st throughout.*

Row 1 (WS): Make a magic ring, ch 1 (does not count as a st), 2 sc into ring. Turn. (2 sts)

Row 2 (RS): Ch 1, 1 sc, 2 sc in last st. Turn. (3 sts)

Row 3: Ch 1, 1 sc, ch 1, sk 1 st, 1 sc. Turn. (2 sts, 1 ch-sp)

Row 4: Ch 1, 1 sc, 1 sc in next ch-sp, ch 1, sk 1 st, 1 sc. Turn. (3 sts, 1 ch-sp)

Row 5: Rep Row 4.

INCREASE SECTION 1

Note: *the increase instructions on Rows 6–37 are marked with curly brackets. When increasing with the pattern repeat in Increase Section 2, you will work the instructions inside these brackets.*

Row 6: Ch 1, 1 sc, {2 esc in sc under next ch-sp, ch 1, sk 1 st, 2 sc in last st. Turn.} (3 sc, 2 esc, 1 ch-sp)

Row 7: Ch 1, 1 sc, {ch 1, 1 sc in next ch-sp, ch 1, sk 2 sts, 1 sc in last st. Turn.} (1 ch-sp increased)

Note: *work all esc into the top V of the esc below.*

Row 8: Ch 1, 1 sc, {2 esc, ch 1, 1 sc in next ch-sp, ch 1, sk 1 st, 1 sc.} Turn. (3 sc, 2 esc, 2 ch-sp)

Row 9: {Ch 1, 1 sc, *1 sc in next ch-sp, ch 1; rep from * to next pair of straight escs,} sk 2 sts, 1 sc. Turn. (1 sc increased)

Row 10: Ch 1, 1 sc, {2 esc, ch 1, 1 sc in next ch-sp, ch 1, sk 1 st, 2 sc in last st.} Turn. (4 sc, 2 esc, 2 ch-sp)

Row 11: {Ch 1, 1sc, *ch 1, 1 sc in next ch-sp; rep from * to next pair of straight escs,} ch 1, sk 2 sts, 1 sc. Turn.} (1 ch-sp increased)

Row 12: Ch 1, 1 sc, {2 esc, *ch 1, 1 sc in next ch-sp; rep from * to last st, ch 1, 1 sc. Turn.} (4 sc, 2 esc, 3 ch-sp)

Row 13: Rep Row 9. (1 sc increased)

Row 14: Ch 1, 1 sc, {2 esc, ch 1, 1 sc in next ch-sp, ch 1, 2 esc in sc under next ch-sp, ch 1, sk 1 st, 2 sc in last st. Turn.} (4 sc, 4 esc, 3 ch-sp)

Row 15: Rep Row 11. (1 ch-sp increased)

Row 16: Ch 1, 1 sc, {2 esc, ch 1, 1 esc in next esc, ch 1, 1 sc in next ch-sp, ch 1, 1 esc in next esc, ch 1, 1 sc in last st. Turn.} (3 sc, 4 esc, 4 ch-sp)

Row 17: Rep Row 9. (1 sc increased)

Row 18: Ch 1, 1 sc, {2 esc, ch 1, 1 esc, ch 1, 1 sc in next ch-sp, ch 1, 1 esc, ch 1, sk 1 st, 2 sc in last st. Turn.} (4 sc, 4 esc, 4 ch-sp)

Row 19: Rep Row11. (1 ch-sp increased)

Row 20: Ch 1, 1 sc, {2 esc, ch 1, 1 sc in next ch-sp, ch 1, 1 esc in esc under ch-sp just worked, 1 esc in next esc, ch 1, 1 sc in ch-sp above esc just worked, ch 1, 1 sc in ch-sp, ch 1, 1 sc in last st. Turn.} (5 sc, 4 esc, 5 ch-sp)

Row 21: Rep Row 9. (1 sc increased)

Row 22: Ch 1, 1 sc, {2 esc, ch 1, 1 sc in next ch-sp, ch 1, 2 esc, ch 1, 1 sc in next ch-sp, sk 1 st, bobble st in next ch-sp, ch 1, sk 1 st, 2 sc in last st. Turn.} (5 sc, 4 esc, 1 bobble, 4 ch-sp)

Row 23: {Ch 1, 1 sc, ch 1, 1 sc in next ch-sp, ch 1, 1 sc in space between bobble st and next sc, ch 1, *1 sc in next ch-sp, ch 1; rep from * to to next pair of straight escs}, sk 2 sts, 1 sc. Turn. (7 sc, 6 ch-sp)

Row 24: Ch 1, 1 sc, {2 esc, ch 1, 1 esc in next esc, ch 1, 1 sc in next ch-sp, ch 1, 1 esc in next esc, *ch 1, 1 sc in next ch-sp; rep from * to last st, ch 1, 1 sc. Turn.} (5 sc, 4 esc, 6 ch-sp)

Row 25: Rep Row 9. (1 sc increased)

Row 26: Ch 1, 1 sc, {2 esc, ch 1, 1 esc, ch 1, 1 sc in next ch-sp, ch 1, 1 esc, *ch 1, 1 sc in next ch-sp; twice, ch 1, sk 1 st, 2 sc in last st. Turn.} (6 sc, 4 esc, 6 ch-sp)

Row 27: Rep Row 11. (1 ch-sp increased)

Row 28: Ch 1, 1 sc, {2 esc, ch 1, 1 sc in next ch-sp, ch 1, 1 esc in esc under ch-sp just worked, 1 esc in next esc, ch 1, 1 sc in ch-sp above esc just worked, *ch 1, 1 sc in next ch-sp; rep from * to last st, ch 1, 1 sc. Turn.} (7 sc, 4 esc, 7 ch-sp)

Row 29: Rep Row 9. (1 sc increased)

Row 30: Ch 1, 1 sc, {2 esc, ch 1, 1 sc in next ch-sp, ch 1, 2 esc, ch 1, 1 sc in next ch-sp, sk 1 st, bobble st in next ch-sp, ch 1, 1 sc in next ch-sp, 2 esc, ch 1, sk 1 st, 2 sc in last st. Turn.} (6 sc, 6 esc, 1 bobble, 6 ch-sp)

Row 31: {Ch 1, work Row 2 of Pattern Repeat once}, 1 sc in last st. Turn. (9 sc, 8 ch-sp)

Row 32: Ch 1, 1 sc, {work Row 3 of Pattern Repeat once, 1 sc in last st. Turn.} (5 sc, 6 esc, 8 ch-sp)

Row 33: {Ch 1, 1 sc, work Row 4 of Pattern Repeat once}, 1 sc in last st. Turn. (1 sc increased)

Row 34: Ch 1, 1 sc, {work Row 5 of Pattern Repeat once, 2 sc in last st. Turn.} (6 sc, 6 esc, 8 ch-sp)

Row 35: {Ch 1, 1 sc, ch 1, work Row 6 of Pattern Repeat once}, 1 sc in last st. (1 ch-sp increased)

Row 36: Ch 1, 1 sc, {work Row 7 of Pattern Repeat once, 1 sc in next ch-sp, ch 1, 1 sc in last st. Turn.} (8 sc, 6 esc, 9 ch-sp)

Row 37: {Ch 1, 1 sc, 1 sc in next ch-sp, ch 1, work Row 8 of Pattern Repeat once}, 1 sc in last st. Turn. (1 sc increased)

INCREASE SECTION 2

In this section, you will repeat Rows 1–8 of the Pattern Repeat together with the bracketed increase instructions from Rows 6–37, as follows:

Row 38 (RS): Ch 1, 1 sc, work Row 1 of Pattern Repeat once, work Row 6 repeat instructions. (7 sc, 8 esc, 1 bobble, 8 ch-sp)

Row 39 (WS): Work Row 7 repeat instructions, work Row 2 of Pattern Repeat once, 1 sc in last st. Turn. (11 sc, 10 ch-sp)

Rows 40–69: Continue as established, working repeat instructions from Rows 8–37. (19 sc, 17 ch-sp)

INCREASE SECTION 3

Rows 70–101: Continue as established, working 2 Pattern Repeat panels before the increase instructions from Rows 6–37. (27 sc, 25 ch-sp)

At the end of this section, you will have 3 full Pattern Repeat panels across the width of the shawl.

INCREASE SECTION 4

Row 102–133: Continue as established, working 3 Pattern Repeat panels before the increase instructions from Rows 6–37. (35 sc, 33 ch-sp)

At the end of this section, you will have 4 full Pattern Repeat panels across the width of the shawl.

INCREASE SECTION 5

Rows 134–149: Continue as established, working repeat instructions from Rows 6–21 and working the 8-row pattern repeat twice in total. (39 sc, 37 ch-sp)

DECREASE SECTION

The shawl decreases are worked at the beginning of WS rows by skipping the first sc. When a pair of escs is worked in front of the last ch-sp of a row, work them together.

Decrease Row 1 (WS): Ch 1, sk first st, 1 sc in first ch-sp, ch 1, *1 sc in next ch-sp, ch 1; rep from * to last st, 1 sc. Turn. (1 st decreased)

Decrease Row 2 (RS): Ch 1, 1 sc, continue in pattern as est to last st, 1 sc. Turn.

Decrease Row 3: Ch 1, sk first st, 1 sc, *1 sc in next ch-sp, ch 1; rep from * to last st, 1 sc. Turn. (1 st decreased)

Decrease Row 4: Ch 1, 1 sc, continue in pattern as est to last ch-sp, 1 sc in last ch-sp, 1 sc. Turn.

On RS rows where 2 esc are worked in front of last ch-sp, work Decrease Row 1 (esc2tog) as follows:

Decrease Row 1 (esc2tog): Ch 1, 1 sc, continue with pattern as est to last 2 esc, esc2tog, ch 1, sk 1 st, 1 sc. Turn. (1 st decreased)

Continue working Decrease Rows until last set of esc sts has been decreased. (3 sts, 1 ch-sp)

Next Row (WS): Ch 1, sk first st, 1 sc in ch-sp, ch 1, 1 sc. Turn.

Next Row (RS): Ch 1, 1 sc in first st, 1 sc in ch-sp, 1 sc in last st. Turn. (3 sts)

Next row: Ch 1, sk first st, 2 sc. Turn. (2 sts)

Final row: Ch 1, 1 sc2tog. (1 st)

Fasten off and weave in ends.

FINISHING

Wet block your shawl to the finished measurements. Once damp, lay it out on a flat surface. Make sure all edges are straight, to set the triangular shape. Pin in place and allow to dry completely.

CHART INSTRUCTIONS

BEGINNING AND SET-UP

Rows 1–7: Work Chart A Rows 1–7. (3 sc, 2 esc, 1 ch-sp)

INCREASE SECTION 1

Rows 8–37: Work Chart A Rows 8–37. (8 sc, 6 esc, 10 ch-sp)

INCREASE SECTION 2

Chart B represents one full set of the 8-row pattern repeat. The gray stitches below Row 1 correspond with Row 37 of Chart A and Row 8 of Chart B. In this section you will continue to work 1 full pattern of Chart B and continue to increase as established on Chart A.

Row 38: Work Chart B Row 1, then work repeat section of Chart A Row 8. (7 sc, 8 esc, 1 bobble, 8 ch-sp)

Row 39: Work repeat section of Chart A Row 9, then work Chart B Row 2. (11 sc, 10 ch-sp)

Rows 40–69: Continue as established, working Chart B Rows 3–8, then repeating Chart B Rows 1–8, while working the repeat section of Chart A Rows 10–37. (19 sc, 17 ch-sp)

INCREASE SECTION 3

Row 70: Work Chart B Row 1, then the repeat section of Chart B Row 1, then the repeat section of Chart A Row 8.

Row 71: Continue as established, working Chart B Rows 2–8, then repeating Chart B Rows 1–8, while working the repeat section of Chart A Rows 10–37. (27 sc, 25 ch-sp)

INCREASE SECTION 4

Rows 102–133: Continue as established in last increase section, working repeats of Chart B and increasing using the repeat section of Chart A Rows 8–37. (35 sc, 33 ch-sp)

INCREASE SECTION 5

Rows 134–149: Continue as established, working repeats of Chart B and increasing using the repeat section of Chart A Rows 3–21. (39 sc, 37 ch-sp)

You now have 4 full pattern repeats, and 1 half pattern repeat.

DECREASE SECTION

Row 150: Work Chart B repeats as set until final double esc, then work repeat section of Chart C Row 15.

Row 151: Work repeat section of Chart C Row 16, then work Chart B as set to end. (39 sc, 36 ch-sp)

Continue as established, working repeats of Chart B and decreasing using the repeat section of Chart C Rows 17–32 once, then Chart C Rows 1–32 until 3 sc remain.

Work Rows 33–35 of Chart C, fasten off and weave in ends.

FINISHING

See written instructions.

CHART A

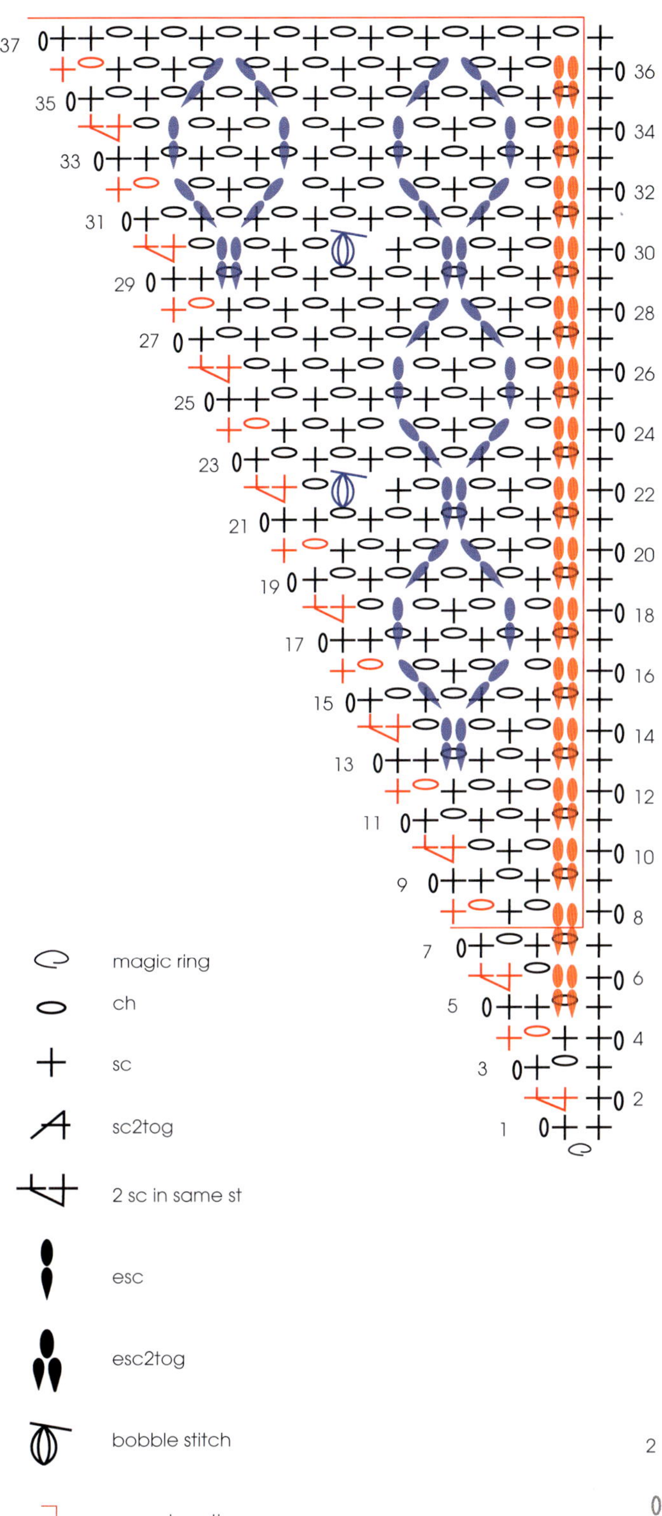

CHART B

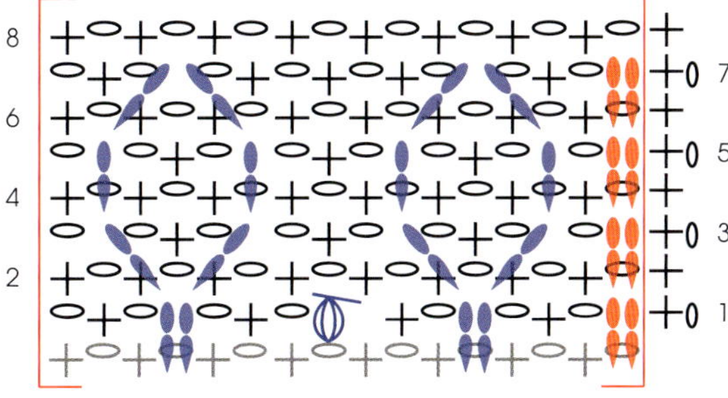

CHART C

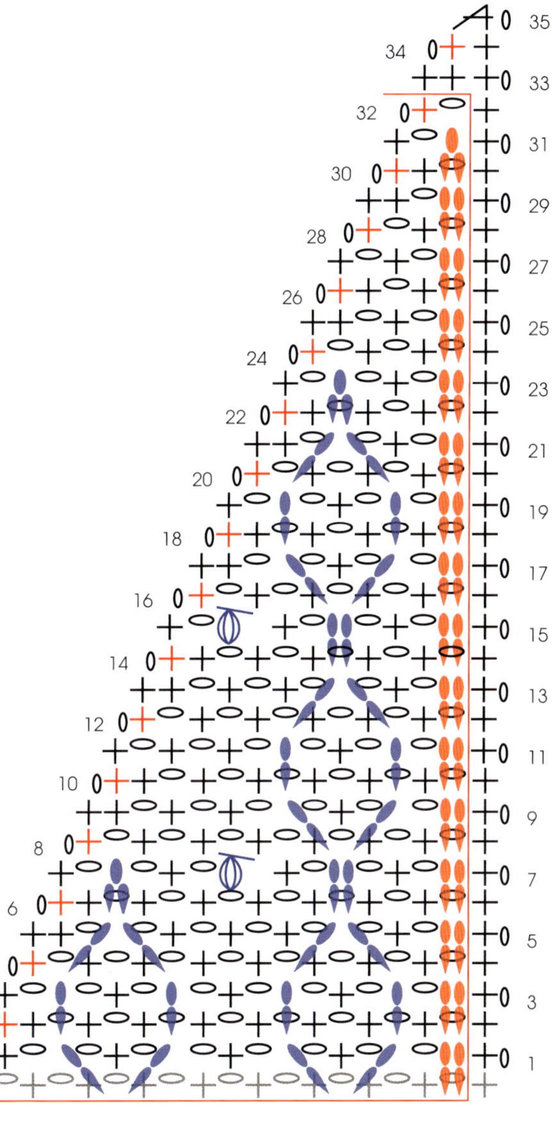

CHAPTER 5:

CROCHET CABLES

This technique creates cables using the simplest crochet stitch – the single crochet – along with its variations: foundation single crochet and extended single crochet.

Each cable is worked sideways and consists of twisted, interlocking waves. To achieve this effect, the yarn is carried through the arches of the waves as you progress; it naturally unravels on the way back when working the next row in the opposite direction, so there's no need to cut the yarn.

Each cable consists of waves and features either a front or back twist. Each wave (W) is made up of single crochet ridges (R) with curved arches of varying stitch counts (S), depending on the design. For example, a C9S/W2/R1 means it is made up of two waves with one ridge in each, and each arch consists of nine stitches. Single cables with different twists are combined to create a double cable, which is twice as wide and has a more complex look.

I strongly recommend starting with the first simple cables, which include detailed instructions and illustrations on twisting the waves and carrying the yarn correctly.

STITCH FOCUS:
Foundation single crochet (fsc)

NOTES ON TECHNIQUE

See General Techniques: Basic Stitches for standard foundation single crochet (fsc) instructions.

You will work the first fsc of each arch into an extended single crochet (esc), and when you have finished the arch, you will work a joining fsc into the next stitch of the ridge.

SPECIAL STITCHES

Fsc into esc: Insert hook into chain of the esc (A), yo and pull up a loop (2 loops on hook), yo and draw through 1 loop, (this creates chain into which you'll work the next fsc), yo and draw through both loops on hook (B).

Joining fsc: Insert hook into ch of last fsc, yo and pull up a loop (2 loops on hook), insert hook under both loops of indicated st, yo and pull up a loop (3 loops on hook) (C), yo and draw through all 3 loops on hook.

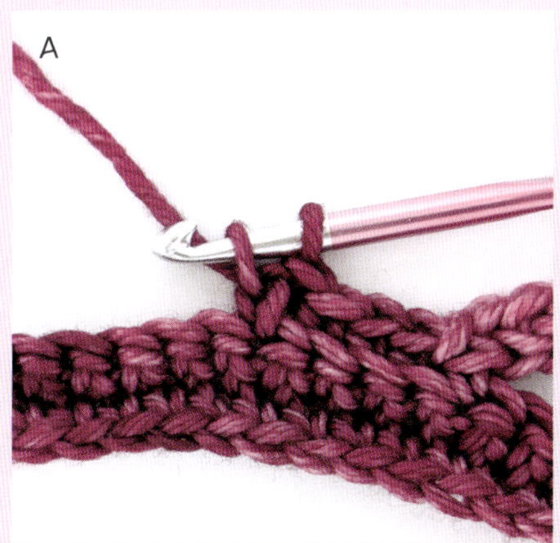
A

Insert the hook into the chain of the esc.

B

After creating the chain of the fsc, yarn over and draw through two loops on hook to finish the stitch.

C

Three loops on hook – one from the previous st, one from the ch of the previous st and one from the next st.

TIGHT TWISTS 1 (C9S/2W/1R/B)

Single cable with 2 waves, each with 1 ridge and 9 stitches per arch, and back twists.

Note: *this cable is worked over a multiple of 10 sts plus 3. Starting chains do not count as sts throughout.*

Start: Chain a multiple of 10 plus 4, with a minimum of 24 sts.

Row 1 (WS): 1 sc in back ridge (bump) of second ch from hook, 1 sc in back ridge (bump) of each ch to end. Turn.

Row 2 (RS): Ch 1, 1 sc BLO in each st to last st, 1 sc. Turn.

WAVE 1

Row 3: Ch 1, 3 sc BLO, 1 esc, *9 fsc, sk 5 sts, 1 joining fsc in next st, 3 sc BLO, 1 esc; rep from * to last 9 sts, 9 fsc, sk 5 sts, 1 joining fsc in next st, 2 sc BLO, 1 sc. Turn.

Row 4: Ch 1, 2 sc BLO, sc2tog BLO, *7 sc BLO, PM, 2 sc BLO, sc2tog BLO, 1 sc BLO, sc2tog BLO; rep from * to last arch, 7 sc BLO, PM, 2 sc BLO, sc2tog BLO, 1 sc BLO, 1 sc. Turn.

Note: *when working in front of the arches, pull the working yarn through from the back of the arches of Wave 1 (C). Before joining them to the base, make sure all the yarn strands you pull through are behind your work. When working the next row, your yarn should unravel from all the arches.*

Wave 1, Rows 1–4

After completing the first four rows, your work should look like this.

Wave 2, Row 5

After working the partial arch, work behind the arch into the 5 skipped sts under the arch of Wave 1.

Before starting the next arch, remove the loop from the hook, bring it in front of the work and reinsert the hook. Pull the working yarn through from the back while working in front of the arch.

WAVE 2

Row 5: Ch 1, 1 esc, 5 fsc (partial arch), working behind arch (into skipped sts from last wave (B)) 1 joining fsc, 3 sc BLO, 1 esc, *remove hook from loop, bring loop in front of arch (C), reinsert hook, 9 fsc (D), working behind arch (into skipped sts from last wave) 1 joining fsc, 3 sc BLO, 1 esc (E); rep from * to last arch, remove and reinsert hook as before and working in front of last arch 5 fsc (partial arch), 1 joining fsc.

Note: *on Row 6, remove and reinsert hook as necessary when working under arches (F).*

Row 6: Ch 1, 4 sc BLO, PM, 2 sc BLO, sc2tog BLO, 1 sc BLO, sc2tog BLO, *7 sc BLO, PM, 2 sc BLO, sc2tog BLO, 1 sc BLO, sc2tog BLO; rep from * to last 6 sts, 5 sc BLO, 1 sc. Turn.

JOINING

Row 7: Ch 1, 4 sc BLO, *1 sc BLO in next marked st, remove M, 4 sc BLO; rep from * to last M, 1 sc BLO of marked st, remove M, 2 sc BLO, 1 sc. Turn.

Row 8: Ch 1, 1 sc BLO in each st to last st, 1 sc.

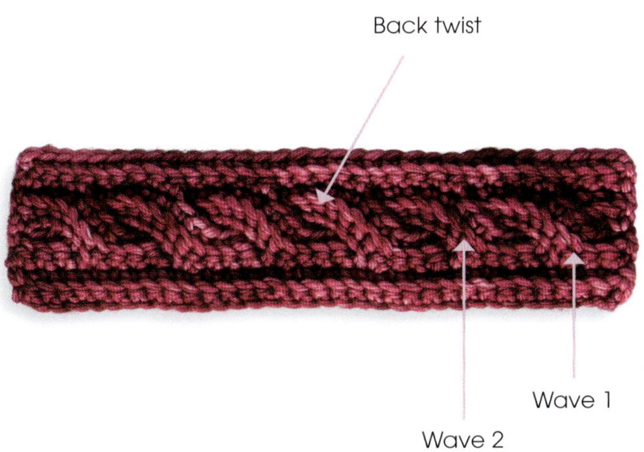

Work 9 fsc of the next arch.

As you go, pull enough working yarn through the arch that you can crochet comfortably.

After completing 9 fsc, work the next 5 sts behind the arches of Wave 1, twisting the new arches you create around the arches of Wave 1.

Make sure the working yarn is always behind your current stitches and hook, so it is pulled only through the arches of Wave 1.

In the next row, working in the opposite direction, remove and reinsert hook as necessary when working under arches.

TIGHT TWISTS 2 (C9S/2W/1R/F)

Single cable with 2 waves, each with 1 ridge and 9 stitches per arch, and wave 1 twists moving from back to front.

Note: *this pattern is worked over a multiple of 10 sts plus 3. Starting chains do not count as sts throughout.*

Start: Chain a multiple of 10 plus 4, with a minimum of 24 sts.

Row 1 (WS): 1 sc in back ridge (bump) of each ch to end. Turn.

Row 2 (RS): Ch 1, 1 sc in BLO in each st to last st, 1 sc. Turn.

WAVE 1

Row 3: Ch 1, 3 sc BLO, 1 esc, *9 fsc, sk 5 sts, 1 joining fsc, 3 sc BLO, 1 esc; rep from * to last 9 sts, 9 fsc, sk 5 sts, 1 joining fsc, 2 sc BLO, 1 sc. Turn.

Row 4: Ch 1, 2 sc BLO, sc2tog BLO, *7 sc BLO, PM, 2 sc BLO, sc2tog BLO, 1 sc BLO, sc2tog BLO; rep from * to last arch, 7 sc BLO, PM, 2 sc BLO, sc2tog BLO, 1 sc BLO, 1 sc. Turn.

WAVE 2

Note: *when working behind the arches, pull the working yarn through from the front of the arches of Wave 1 (C). Before joining them to the base, make sure all the yarn strands you pull through are in front of your work. When working the next row, your yarn should unravel from all the arches.*

A

Wave 1, Rows 1–4

The only difference between C9S/2W/1R/B and C9S/2W/1R/F is that the new arches will be twisting around the First wave arches from back to front, and the working yarn will be left in front of your work and hook.

B

Wave 2, Row 5

After working the partial arch, work in front of the arch into the 5 skipped sts under the arch of Wave 1.

C

Remove and reinsert your hook, bring loop behind your work. Work the next 9 fsc.

Row 5: Ch 1, 1 esc, 5 fsc (partial arch), working in front of arch into skipped sts from last wave (B) 1 joining fsc, 3 sc BLO, 1 esc, *remove hook from loop, bring loop behind arch (C), reinsert hook, 9 fsc (D), working in front of arch (into skipped sts from last wave) 1 joining fsc, 3 sc BLO, 1 esc (E); rep from * to last arch, remove and reinsert hook as before and working behind last arch 5 fsc, 1 joining fsc.

Note: *on Row 6, remove and reinsert hook as necessary when working under arches (F).*

Row 6: Ch 1, 4 sc BLO, PM, 2 sc BLO, sc2tog BLO, 1 sc BLO, sc2tog BLO, *7 sc BLO, PM, 2 sc BLO, sc2tog BLO, 1 sc BLO, sc2tog BLO* rep from * to last partial arch, 5 sc BLO, 1 sc. Turn.

JOINING

Row 7: Ch 1, 4 sc BLO, *1 sc BLO in next marked st, remove M, 4 sc BLO; rep from * to last M, 1 sc BLO in marked st, remove M, 2 sc BLO, 1 sc. Turn.

Row 8: Ch 1, 1 sc BLO in each st to last st, 1 sc.

As you now wrap the new arches from back to front, the working yarn should always stay in front of your work and hook for the second cable. Work next 5 sts under the next arch.

Take a look at how the yarn is pulled through for the second cable: it always stays in front of the sts and arches of the current row (opposite to the first cable).

In the next row, working in the opposite direction, remove and reinsert hook as necessary when working under arches.

Your yarn should be unraveled from all the arches if fed through properly on the previous row.

GENTLE WAVES (C11S/2W/1R)

Single cable with 2 waves, each with 1 ridge and 11 stitches per arch.

These cables are more airy and open than the 9-st cables. Depending on the chosen twist and the orientation of the final fabric, the cables can look quite different.

While the back twist is generally easier, a front twist can enhance the cable's definition, giving the waves a more distinct and polished look.

Note: *this cable is worked over a multiple of 12 sts plus 7. Starting chains do not count as sts throughout.*

Start: Chain a multiple of 12 plus 8 with a minimum of 32 sts.

Row 1 (WS): 1 sc in back ridge (bump) of second ch from hook, 1 sc in back ridge (bump) of each ch to end. Turn.

Row 2 (RS): Ch 1, 1 sc BLO in each st to last st, 1 sc. Turn.

WAVE 1

Row 3: Ch 1, 5 sc BLO, 1 esc, 11 fsc, *sk 7 sts, 1 joining fsc, 3 sc BLO, 1 esc, 11 fsc; rep from * to last 13 sts, sk 7 sts, 1 joining fsc, 4 sc BLO, 1 hdc. Turn.

Row 4: Ch 1, 3 sc BLO, *sk 1 st, 10 sc BLO, PM, 5 sc BLO; rep from * to last 4 sts, sk 1 st, 2 sc BLO, 1 hdc. Turn.

WAVE 2

Row 5: Ch 1, 1 sc BLO, 1 esc, 7 fsc (partial arch), *using either a front or a back twist here and throughout, sk first st under next arch, 1 joining fsc, 3 sc BLO, 1 esc, 11 fsc; rep from * to last arch, sk first st under last arch, 1 joining fsc, 3 sc BLO, 1 esc, 7 fsc, working into last 2 sts of prev row 1 joining fsc, 1 hdc. Turn.

Row 6: Ch 1, 6 sc BLO, PM, 5 sc BLO, *sk 1 st, 10 sc BLO, PM, 5 sc BLO; rep from * to last 12 sts, skip 1 st, 10 sc BLO, 1 hdc. Turn.

JOINING

Row 7: Ch 1, 6 sc BLO, *ch 1, 1 sc BLO in next marked st, remove M, 4 sc BLO, rep from * to last st, 1 sc. Turn.

Row 8: Ch 1, sc BLO in each st and ch to last st, 1 sc.

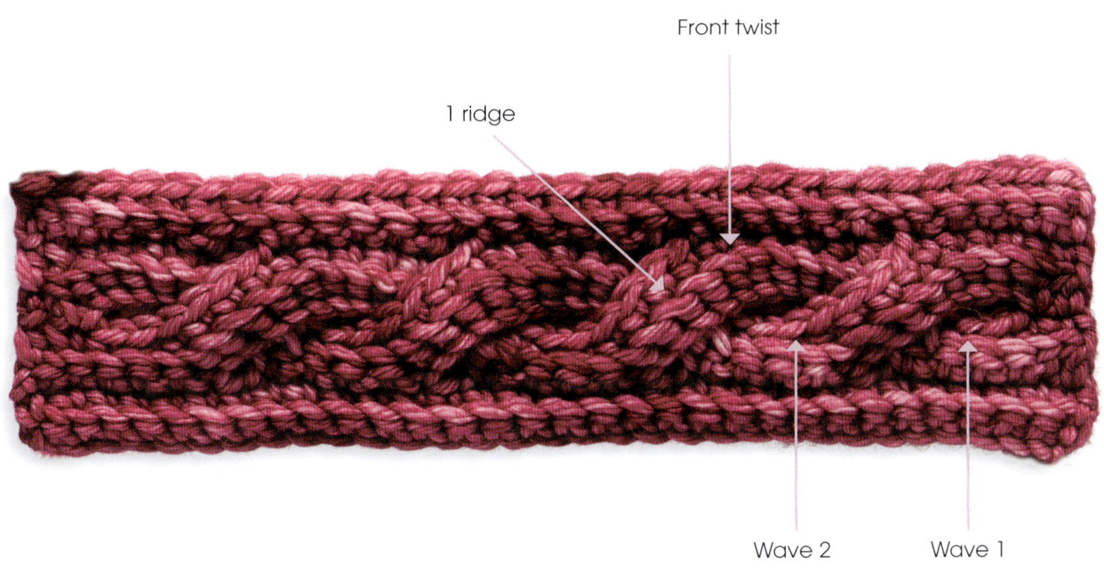

TRAVELING VINES (DOUBLE C11S/2W/1R)

Double cable consisting of 2 single cables of 2 waves, each with 1 ridge and 11 stitches per arch, with the front and back twists worked together.

This double cable is twice as wide as the singles, and even airier. You can adjust the order of the twists (starting with the back twist and finishing with the front twist, or vice versa) depending on the direction of your fabric and the desired cable orientation.

Note: *this cable is worked over a multiple of 12 sts plus 7. Starting chains do not count as sts throughout.*

Start: Chain a multiple of 12 plus 8 with a minimum of 32 sts.

Row 1 (WS): 1 sc in back ridge (bump) of second ch from hook, 1 sc in back ridge (bump) of each ch to end. Turn.

Row 2 (RS): Ch 1, 1 sc BLO in each st to last st, 1 sc. Turn.

WAVE 1

Rows 3 and 4: Work as for C11S/2W/1R.

WAVE 2

Row 5: Ch 1, 1 sc BLO, 1 esc, 7 fsc, *using a Front twist sk first st under arch, 1 joining fsc, 3 sc BLO, 1 esc, 11 fsc; rep from * to last arch, sk first st under last arch, 1 joining fsc, 3 sc BLO, 1 esc, 7 fsc, working in last 2 sts of prev row 1 joining fsc, 1 hdc. Turn.

Row 6: Ch 1, 6 sc BLO, PM, 5 sc BLO, *sk 1 st, 10 sc BLO, PM, 5 sc BLO; rep from * to last 12 sts, sk 1 st, 10 sc BLO, 1 hdc. Turn.

WAVE 3

Row 7: Ch 1, 5 sc BLO, 1 esc, 11 fsc, *sk 1 M, 1 joining fsc in next marked st, remove M, 3 sc BLO, 1 esc, 11 fsc; rep from * to last 2 M, sk 1 M, 1 joining fsc in next marked st, remove M, 4 sc BLO, 1 hdc. Turn.

Row 8: Ch 1, 3 sc BLO, *sk 1 st, 10 sc BLO, PM, 5 sc BLO; rep from * to last 4 sts, sk 1 st, 2 sc BLO, 1 hdc. Turn.

WAVE 4

Row 9: Ch 1, 1 sc BLO, 1 esc, 7 fsc, *using a Back twist and working into sts of Wave 2, 1 joining fsc in next marked st of Wave 2, remove M, 3 sc BLO, 1 esc, 11 fsc; rep from * to last M, 1 joining fsc in next marked st of Wave 2, 3 sc BLO, 1 esc, 7 fsc, working in last 2 sts of prev row 1 joining fsc, 1 hdc. Turn.

Row 10: Ch 1, 6 sc BLO, PM, 5 sc BLO, *sk 1 st, 10 sc BLO, 5 sc BLO; rep from * to last 12 sts, sk 1 st, 10 sc BLO, 1 hdc. Turn.

JOINING

Row 11: Ch 1, 6 sc BLO, *ch 1, 1 sc BLO in next marked st, remove M, 4 sc BLO; rep from * to last st, 1 sc. Turn.

Row 12: Ch 1, sc BLO in each st and ch to last st, 1 sc.

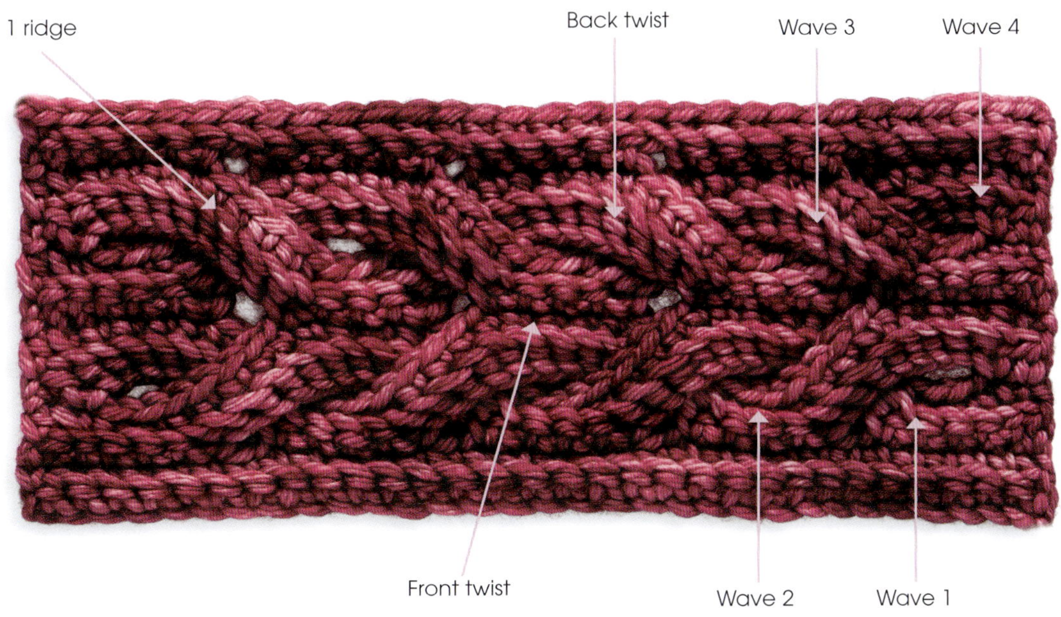

GENTLE CURVES (C11S/2W/2R)

Single cable with 2 waves, each with 2 ridges and 11 stitches per arch.

These cables are well-defined and textured, yet lie quite flat without added bulk, making them ideal for projects that need a refined texture.

Note: *this cable is worked over a multiple of 12 sts plus 7. Starting chains do not count as sts throughout.*

Start: Chain a multiple of 12 plus 8 with a minimum of 32 sts.

Row 1 (WS): 1 sc in back ridge (bump) of second ch from hook, 1 sc in back ridge (bump) of each ch to end. Turn.

Row 2 (RS): Ch 1, 1 sc BLO in each st to last st, 1 sc. Turn.

WAVE 1

Row 3: Ch 1, 5 sc BLO, 1 esc, 11 fsc, *sk 7 sts, 1 joining fsc, 3 sc BLO, 1 esc, 11 fsc; rep from * to last 13 sts, sk 7 sts, 1 joining fsc, 4 sc BLO, 1 sc. Turn.

Row 4: Ch 1, 3 sc BLO, sk 1 st, 1 sc BLO in each st to last 4 sts, sk 1 st, 2 sc BLO, 1 sc. Turn.

Row 5: Ch 1, 1 sc BLO in each st to last st, 1 sc. Turn.

Row 6: Ch 1, 3 sc BLO, sk 1 st, 10 sc BLO, *16 sc BLO, PM; rep from * to last 7 sts, 3 sc BLO, sk 1 st, 2 sc BLO, 1 sc. Turn.

WAVE 2

Row 7: Ch 1, 1 sc BLO, 1 esc, 8 fsc, *using either a front or a back twist, sk first st under next arch, 1 joining fsc, 3 sc BLO, 1 esc, 11 fsc; rep from * to last arch, sk first st under last arch, 1 joining fsc, 3 sc BLO, 1 esc, 6 fsc, working in last 2 sts of prev row 1 joining fsc, 1 sc. Turn.

Rows 8 and 9: Rep Row 5.

Row 10: Ch 1, 6 sc BLO, PM, *16 sc BLO, PM; rep from * to last st, 1 sc. Turn.

JOINING

Row 11: Ch 1, 6 sc BLO, *ch 1, 1 sc BLO in next marked st, remove M, 4 sc BLO, rep from * to last st, 1 sc. Turn.

Row 12: Ch 1, 1 sc BLO in each st and ch to last st, 1 sc.

BOLD BRAIDS (DOUBLE C11S/2W/2R)

Double cable consisting of 2 single 2-wave cables, each with 2 ridges and 11 stitches per arch, with the front and back twists worked together.

This double cable is bold and richly textured, ideal for statement pieces.

Note: *this cable is worked over a multiple of 12 sts plus 7. Starting chains do not count as sts throughout.*

Start: Chain a multiple of 12 plus 8 with a minimum of 32 sts.

Row 1 (WS): 1 sc in back ridge (bump) of second ch from hook, 1 sc in back ridge (bump) of each ch to end. Turn.

Row 2 (RS): Ch 1, 1 sc BLO in each st to last st, 1 sc. Turn.

WAVE 1

Row 3: Ch 1, 5 sc BLO, 1 esc, 11 fsc, *sk 7 sts, 1 joining fsc, 3 sc BLO, 1 esc, 11 fsc; rep from * to last 13 sts, sk 7 sts, 1 joining fsc, 4 sc BLO, 1 sc. Turn.

Row 4: Ch 1, 3 sc BLO, sk 1 st, 1 sc BLO in each st to last 4 sts, sk 1 st, 2 sc BLO, 1 sc. Turn.

Row 5: Ch 1, 1 sc BLO in each st to last st, 1 sc. Turn.

Row 6: Ch 1, 3 sc BLO, sk 1 st, 10 sc BLO, PM, *16 sc BLO, PM; rep from * to last 7 sts, 3 sc BLO, sk 1 st, 2 sc BLO, 1 sc. Turn.

WAVE 2

Row 7: Ch 1, 1 sc BLO, 1 esc, 8 fsc, *using a front twist sk first st under arch, 1 joining fsc, 3 sc BLO, 1 esc, 11 fsc; rep from * to last arch, sk first st under last arch, 1 joining fsc, 3 sc BLO, 1 esc, 6 fsc, working in last 2 sts of prev row 1 joining fsc, 1 sc. Turn.

Rows 8 and 9: Rep Row 5.

Row 10: Ch 1, 6 sc BLO, PM, *16 sc BLO, PM; rep from * to last st, 1 sc. Turn.

WAVE 3

Row 11: Ch 1, 5 sc BLO, 1 esc, 11 fsc, *sk 1 M, 1 joining fsc in next marked st, remove M, 3 sc BLO, 1 esc, 11 fsc; rep from * to last 2 M, sk 1 M, 1 joining fsc in next marked st, 4 sc BLO, 1 sc. Turn.

Rows 12–14: Rep Rows 4–6.

WAVE 4

Row 15: Ch 1, 1 sc BLO, 1 esc, 8 fsc, *using a back twist and working into sts of Wave 2 work 1 joining fsc in next marked st, 3 sc BLO, 1 esc, 11 fsc; rep from * to last M of Wave 2, 1 joining fsc in next marked st of Wave 2, 3 sc in BLO, 1 esc, 6 fsc, working in last 2 sts of prev row work 1 joining fsc, 1 sc. Turn.

Rows 16–18: Rep Rows 8–10.

JOINING

Row 19: Ch 1, 6 sc BLO, *ch 1, 1 sc BLO in next marked st, 4 sc BLO; rep from * to last st, 1 sc. Turn.

Row 20: Ch 1, sc BLO in each st and ch to last st, 1 sc.

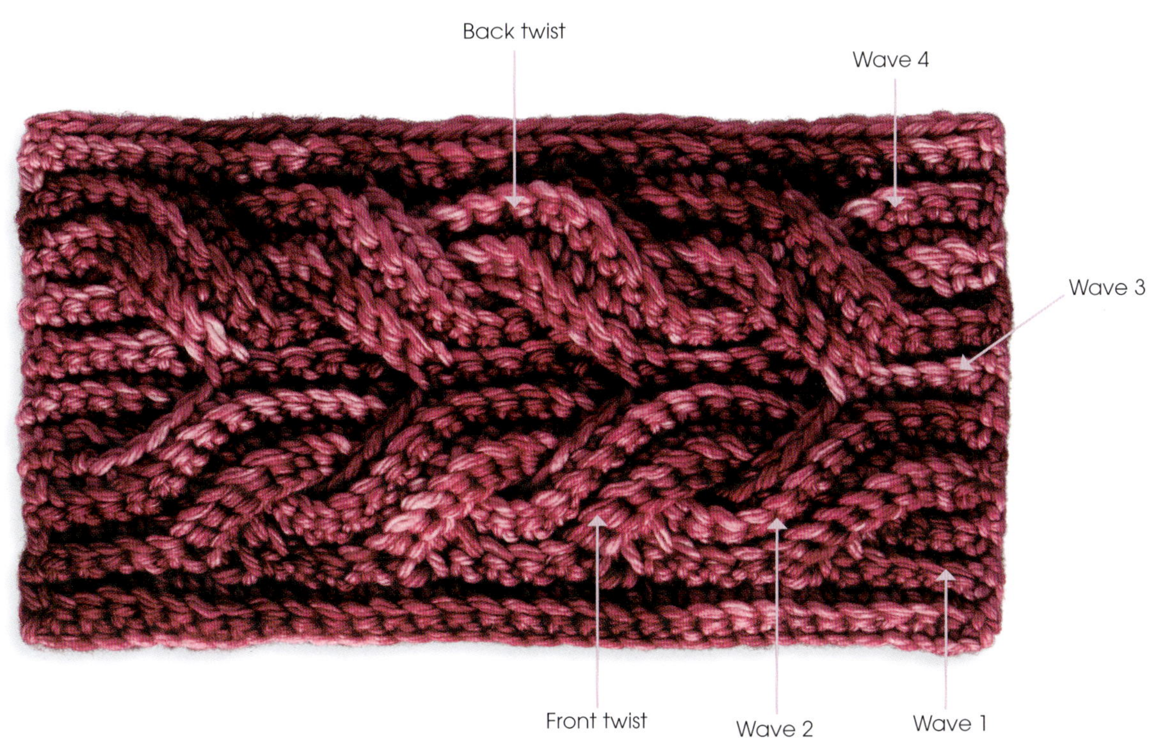

TWINING ROPES (C15S/3W/1R)

Single cable with 3 waves, each with 1 ridge and 15 stitches per arch.

These delicate cables resemble intertwined fiber ropes. The triple twist gives them a substantial thickness, while the open structure of 15-stitch arches keeps them loose and flexible.

Note: *this cable is worked over a multiple of 15 sts plus 1. Starting chains do not count as sts throughout.*

Start: Chain a multiple of 15 plus 2, with a minimum of 32 stitches.

Row 1 (WS): 1 sc in back ridge (bump) of second ch from hook, 1 sc in back ridge (bump) of each ch to end. Turn.

Row 2 (RS): Ch 1, 1 sc BLO in each st to last st, 1 sc. Turn.

WAVE 1

Row 3: Ch 1, 2 sc BLO, 1 esc, 15 fsc, *sk 10 sts, 1 joining fsc, 3 sc BLO, 1 esc, 15 fsc; rep from * to last 13 sts, sk 10 sts, 1 joining fsc, 1 sc BLO, 1 sc. Turn.

Row 4: Ch 1, 11 sc BLO, PM, *20 sc BLO, PM; rep from * to last 10 sts, 9 sc BLO, 1 sc. Turn.

WAVE 2

Row 5: Ch 1, 2 sc BLO, 1 esc, 8 fsc, *using either a front or back twist here and throughout, sk 5 sts under arch, 1 joining fsc, 3 sc BLO, 1 esc, 15 fsc; rep from * to last arch, sk 5 sts under arch, 1 joining fsc, 3 sc BLO, 1 esc, 3 fsc,1 joining fsc in last st of previous row. Turn.

Row 6: Ch 1, 17 sc BLO, PM, *20 sc BLO, PM; rep from * to last 3 sts, 2 sc BLO, 1 sc. Turn.

WAVE 3

Row 7: Ch 1, 1 esc, 5 fsc, *using chosen twist and working in rem sts under arch: 1 joining fsc, 3 sc BLO, 1 esc, 15 fsc; rep from * to last 5 unworked sts under arch, 1 joining fsc, 3 sc BLO, 1 esc, 7 fsc, working in last 3 sts of previous row 1 joining fsc, 1 sc in BLO, 1 sc. Turn.

Row 8: Ch 1, 3 sc BLO, PM, *20 sc BLO, PM; rep from * to last 18 sts, 17 sc BLO, 1 sc. Turn.

JOINING

Row 9: Ch 1, 3 sc BLO, 1 sc BLO in next marked st, Remove M, 4 sc BLO; rep from * to last M, 1 sc BLO in last marked st, remove M, 1 sc BLO, 1 sc. Turn.

Row 10: Ch 1, sc BLO in each st to last st, 1 sc.

BRAIDED ROPES (DOUBLE C15S/3W/1R)

Double cable consisting of 2 single 3-wave cables, each with 1 ridge and 15 stitches per arch, with the front and back twists worked together.

This double cable has a gentle V shape and, like all double cables, it enhances the features of the single cable, creating an even more delicate structure. I recommend using these cables in fabric with a vertical or diagonal orientation as, if placed horizontally, they may stretch under their own weight.

Note: *this cable is worked over a multiple of 15 sts plus 1. Starting chains do not count as sts throughout.*

Start: Chain a multiple of 15 plus 2 with a minimum of 32 stitches.

Row 1 (WS): Row 1 (WS): 1 sc in back ridge (bump) of second ch from hook, 1 sc in back ridge (bump) of each ch to end. Turn.

Row 2 (RS): Ch 1, 1 sc BLO in each st to last st, 1 sc. Turn.

WAVE 1

Row 3: Ch 1, 2 sc BLO, 1 esc, 15 fsc, *sk 10 sts, 1 joining fsc, 3 sc BLO, 1 esc, 15 fsc; rep from * to last 13 sts, sk 10 sts, 1 joining fsc, 1 sc BLO, 1 sc. Turn.

Row 4: Ch 1, 11 sc BLO, PM, *20 sc BLO, PM; rep from * to last 10 sts, 9 sc BLO, 1 sc. Turn.

WAVE 2

Row 5: Ch 1, 2 sc BLO, 1 esc, 8 fsc, *using a back twist sk 5 sts under arch, 1 joining fsc, 3 sc BLO, 1 esc, 15 fsc; rep from * to last arch, sk 5 sts under arch, 1 joining fsc, 3 sc BLO, 1 esc, 3 fsc, 1 joining fsc in last st of prev row. Turn.

Row 6: Ch 1, 17 sc BLO, PM, *20 sc BLO, PM; rep from * to last 3 sts, 2 sc BLO, 1 sc. Turn.

WAVE 3

Row 7: Ch 1, 1 esc, 5 fsc, *using a back twist (1 joining fsc, 3 sc BLO, 1 esc) in 5 unworked sts under arch, 15 fsc; rep from * to last 5 unworked sts under arch, 1 joining fsc, 3 sc BLO, 1 esc, 7 fsc, working in last 3 sts of prev row work 1 joining fsc, 1 sc BLO, 1 sc. Turn.

Row 8: Ch 1, 3 sc BLO, PM, *20 sc BLO, PM; rep from * to last 18 sts, 17 sc BLO, 1 sc. Turn.

WAVE 4

Row 9: Ch 1, 2 sc BLO, 1 esc, 15 fsc, *sk 2 M, working in next marked st and next 4 sts (in Wave 3 arches) work 1 joining fsc, 3 sc BLO, 1 esc, 15 fsc; rep from * to last 3 M, sk 2 M, working in next marked st and last 2 sts work 1 joining fsc, 1 sc BLO, 1 sc. Turn.

Row 10: Ch 1, 15 sc BLO, PM, *20 sc BLO, PM; rep from * to last 6 sts, 5 sc BLO, 1 sc. Turn.

WAVE 5

Row 11: Ch 1, 1 esc, 3 fsc, *using a front twist and working in next marked st and next 4 sts (in Wave 2 arches) work 1 joining fsc, 3 sc BLO, 1 esc, 15 fsc, sk 1 M; rep from * to last 2 M, working in next marked st and next 4 sts work 1 joining fsc, 3 sc BLO, 1 esc, 9 fsc, working in last 3 sts of prev row work 1 joining fsc, 1 sc BLO, 1 sc. Turn.

Row 12: Ch 1, 9 sc BLO, PM, *20 sc BLO, PM; rep from * to last 12 sts, 11 sc BLO, 1 sc. Turn.

WAVE 6

Row 13: Ch 1, 2 sc BLO, 1 esc, 7 fsc, *using a front twist and working in next lowest marked st and next 4 sts (in Wave 1 arches) work 1 joining fsc, 3 sc BLO, 1 esc, 15 fsc, sk 1 M; rep from * to last M of Wave 1, working in next marked st and next 4 sts work 1 joining fsc, 3 sc BLO, 1 esc, 5 fsc, working in last st of prev row work 1 joining fsc. Turn.

Row 14: Ch 1, 3 sc BLO, PM, *20 sc BLO, PM; rep from * to last 18 sts, 17 sc BLO, 1 sc. Turn.

JOINING

Row 15: Ch 1, 3 sc BLO, *working in next marked st and next 4 sts work 5 sc BLO; rep from * to last M, starting from next marked st work 2 sc BLO, 1 sc. Turn.

Row 16: Ch 1, sc BLO in each st to last st, 1 sc.

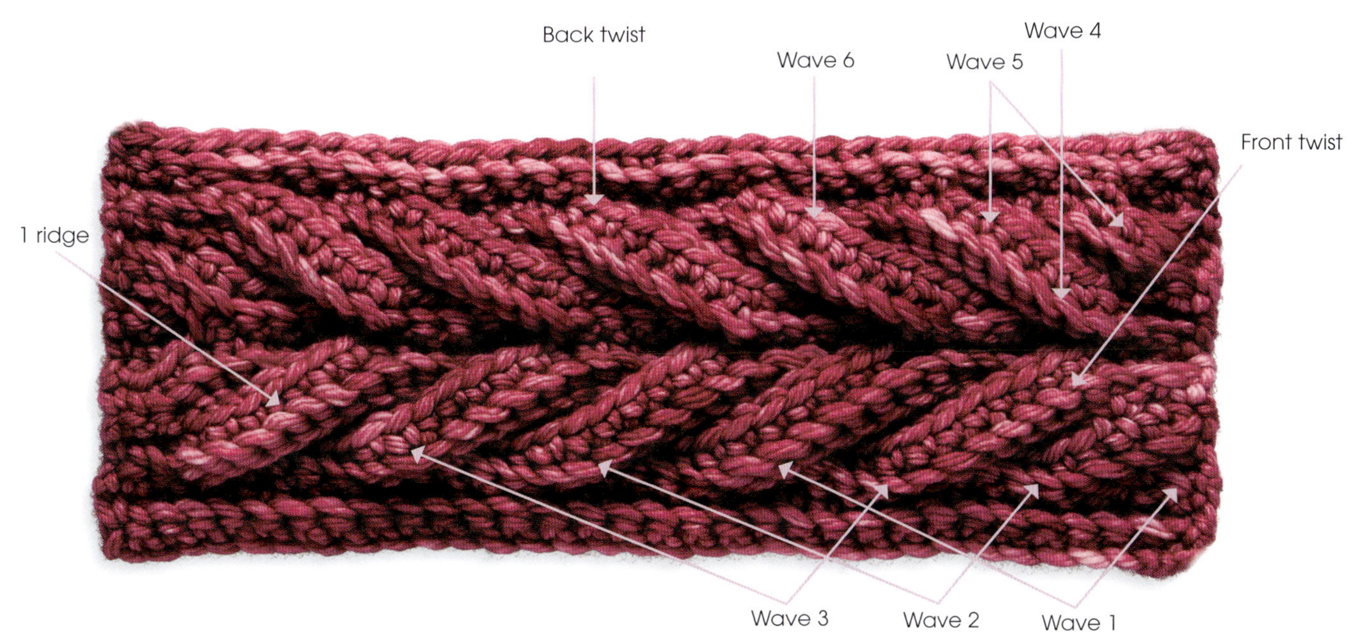

SCULPTED CURVES (C15S/2W/2R/B)

Single cable with 2 waves, each with 2 ridges and 15 stitches per arch, and wave 1 twists moving from front to back.

The bold curves of this cable are achieved using a smart technique from Chapter 3. This method merges the 2-ridge waves into a single ridge at certain points, providing extra definition to the cable. Because of this, the twist cannot simply be reversed in this design – each twist requires its own instructions. The back twist cable instructions are provided in full; to make the front twist cable, see DC15S/2W/2R instructions.

Note: *this cable is worked over a multiple of 12 sts plus 7. Starting chains do not count as sts throughout.*

Start: Chain a multiple of 12 plus 8 with a minimum of 32 stitches.

Row 1 (WS): Row 1 (WS): 1 sc in back ridge (bump) of second ch from hook, 1 sc in back ridge (bump) of each ch to end. Turn.

Row 2 (RS): Ch 1, 1 sc BLO in each st to last st, 1 sc. Turn.

WAVE 1

Row 3: Ch 1, 5 sc BLO, 1 esc, 15 fsc, *sk 7 sts, 1 joining fsc, 3 sc BLO, 1 esc, 15 fsc; rep from * to last 13 sts, sk 7 sts, 1 joining fsc, 4 sc in BLO, 1 sc. Turn.

Row 4: Ch 1, 3 sc BLO, sk 1 st, 2 sc BLO, *ch 6, sk 6 sts, 11 sc BLO, sk 1 st, 2 sc BLO; rep from * to last st, 1 sc. Turn.

Row 5: Ch 1, 1 sc BLO, *13 sc BLO, ch 6, sk ch6-sp; rep from * to last 5 sts, 4 sc BLO, 1 sc. Turn.

Row 6: Ch 1, 4 sc BLO, *sk 1 st, working in front of ch6-sps work 6 sc BLO into 6 skipped sts from Row 4, cont working in sts of prev row work 5 sc BLO, PM, 4 sc BLO, sk 1 st, 2 sc BLO; rep from to last 2 sts, 1 sc BLO, 1 sc. Turn.

WAVE 2

Row 7: Ch 1, 1 sc BLO, 1 esc, 10 fsc, *using back twist, sk first st under arch, 1 joining fsc, 3 sc BLO, 1 esc, 15 fsc; rep from * to last arch, sk first st under arch, 1 joining fsc, 3 sc BLO, 1 esc, 8 fsc, working in last 2 sts of prev row work 1 joining fsc, 1 sc. Turn.

Row 8: Ch 1, 12 sc BLO, sk 1 st, 2 sc BLO, ch 6, sk 6 sts, *11 sc BLO, sk 1 st, 2 sc BLO, ch 6, sk 6 sts; rep from * to last 6 sts, 5 sc BLO, 1 sc. Turn.

Row 9: Ch 1, 6 sc BLO, *ch 6, sk ch6-sp, 13 sc BLO; rep from * to last st, 1 sc. Turn.

Row 10: Ch 1, 6 sc BLO, PM, 4 sc BLO, sk 1 st, 2 sc BLO, sk 1 st, *working in front of ch6-sp work 6 sc BLO into 6 skipped sts from Row 4, cont working in sts of prev row work 5 sc BLO, PM, 4 sc BLO, sk 1 st, 2 sc BLO, sk 1 st; rep from * to last ch6-sp, working in front of 6ch-sps work 6 sc BLO in 6 skipped sts from Row 4, cont working in sts of prev row, work 5 sc BLO, 1 sc. Turn.

JOINING

Row 11: Ch 1, 6 sc BLO, *ch 1, starting from next marked st work 5 sc BLO; rep from * to last st, 1 sc. Turn.

Row 12: Ch 1, sc BLO in each st and ch to last st, 1 sc.

To work the front twist version, work instructions for Waves 1 and 2 of the DC15S/2W/2R, and join using Rows 19 and 20.

DEFINED TWISTS (DOUBLE C15S/2W/2R)

Double cable consisting of 2 single 2-wave cables, each with 2 ridges and 15 stitches per arch, with the front and back twists worked together.

The widest of all the double cables listed, this has an open look, setting it apart from the more solidly twisted 2-ridge double cables. If you need to change the cable's orientation and switch the twists, do not simply reverse the instructions. Instead, work the instructions for the single cable with a back twist first, then continue as directed for a front-twisted cable.

Note: *this cable is worked over a multiple of 12 sts plus 7. Starting chains do not count as sts throughout.*

Start: Chain a multiple of 12 plus 8 with a minimum of 32 stitches.

Row 1 (WS): Row 1 (WS): 1 sc in back ridge (bump) of second ch from hook, 1 sc in back ridge (bump) of each ch to end. Turn.

Row 2 (RS): Ch 1, 1 sc BLO in each st to last st, 1 sc. Turn.

WAVE 1

Row 3: Ch 1, 5 sc BLO, 1 esc, 15 fsc, *sk 7 sts, 1 joining fsc, 3 sc BLO, 1 esc, 15 fsc; rep from * to last 13 sts, sk 7 sts, 1 joining fsc, 4 sc BLO, 1 sc. Turn.

Row 4: Ch 1, 3 sc BLO, sk 1 st, *11 sc BLO, ch 6, sk 6 sts, 2 sc BLO, sk 1 st; rep from * to last 3 sts, 2 sc BLO, 1 sc. Turn.

Row 5: Ch 1, 5 sc BLO, *ch 6, sk ch6-sp, 13 sc BLO; rep from * to last st, 1 sc. Turn.

Row 6: Ch 1, 4 sc BLO, *sk 1 st, 9 sc BLO, PM, working in front of ch6-sp work 6 sc BLO in 6 skipped from Row 4, cont working in sts of prev row, sk 1 st, 2 sc BLO; rep from to last 2 sts, 1 sc BLO, 1 sc. Turn.

WAVE 2

Row 7: Ch 1, 1 sc BLO, 1 esc, 8 fsc, *using a front twist, sk first st under arch, 1 joining fsc, 3 sc BLO, 1 esc, 15 fsc; rep from * to last arch, sk first st under arch, 1 joining fsc, 3 sc BLO, 1 esc, 10 fsc, working in last 2 sts of prev row work 1 joining fsc, 1 sc. Turn.

Row 8: Ch 1, 6 sc BLO, *ch 6, sk 6 sts, 2 sc BLO, sk 1 st, 11 sc BLO; rep from * to last st, 1 sc. Turn.

Row 9: Ch 1, 1 sc BLO, *13 sc BLO, ch 6, sk ch6-sp; rep from * to last 6 sts, 5 sc BLO, 1 sc. Turn.

Row 10: Ch 1, 6 sc BLO, PM, *working in front of ch6-sp work 6 sc BLO in 6 skipped sts from Row 4, sk 1 st, 2 sc BLO, sk 1 st, cont working in sts of prev row work 9 sc BLO, PM; rep from * to last 18 sts, working in front of ch6-sp work 6 sc BLO in 6 skipped sts from Row 4, sk 1 st, 2 sc BLO, sk 1 st, cont working in sts of prev row work 9 sc BLO, 1 sc. Turn.

WAVE 3

Row 11: Ch 1, 5 sc BLO, 1 esc, 15 fsc, *sk 1 M, starting in next marked st of Wave 2 work 1 joining fsc, 3 sc BLO, 1 esc, 15 fsc; rep from * to last 2 M, sk 1 M, working in next marked st and next 5 sts work 1 joining fsc, 4 sc BLO, 1 sc. Turn.

Row 12: Ch 1, 3 sc BLO, sk 1 st, 2 sc BLO, *ch 6, sk 6 sts, 11 sc BLO, sk 1 st, 2 sc BLO; rep from * to last st, 1 sc. Turn.

Row 13: Ch 1, 1 sc BLO, *13 sc BLO, ch 6, skip ch6-sp; rep from * to last 5 sts, 4 sc BLO, 1 sc. Turn.

Row 14: Ch 1, 4 sc in BLO, *sk 1 st, working in front of ch6-sps work 6 sc BLO in 6 skipped sts from Row 4, cont working in sts of prev row work 5 sc BLO, PM, 4 sc BLO, sk 1 st, 2 sc BLO; rep from * to last 2 sts, 1 sc BLO, 1 sc. Turn.

WAVE 4

Row 15: Ch 1, 1 sc BLO, 1 esc, 10 fsc, *using a back twist and starting in next marked st of Wave 1 work 1 joining fsc, 3 sc BLO, 1 esc, 15 fsc; rep from * to last M, 1 joining fsc, 3 sc BLO, 1 esc, 8 fsc, working in last 2 sts of prev row work 1 joining fsc, 1 sc. Turn.

Row 16: Ch 1, 12 sc BLO, sk 1 st, 2 sc BLO, ch 6, sk 6 sts, *11 sc BLO, sk 1 st, 2 sc BLO, ch 6, sk 6 sts; rep from * to last 6 sts, 5 sc BLO, 1 sc. Turn.

Row 17: Ch 1, 6 sc BLO, *ch 6, sk ch6-sp, 13 sc BLO; rep from * to last st, 1 sc. Turn.

Row 18: Ch 1, 6 sc BLO, PM, 4 sc BLO, sk 1 st, 2 sc BLO, sk 1 st, *working in front of ch6-sp work 6 sc BLO in 6 skipped sts from Row 4, cont working in sts of prev row, work 5 sc BLO, PM, 4 sc BLO, sk 1 st, 2 sc BLO, sk 1 st; rep from * to last ch6-sp, working in front of ch6-sp work 6 sc BLO in 6 skipped 6 sts from Row 4, cont working in sts of prev row, work 5 sc BLO, 1 sc. Turn.

JOINING

Row 19: Ch 1, 6 sc BLO, *ch 1, starting from next marked st work 5 sc BLO; rep from * to last st, 1 sc. Turn.

Row 20: Ch 1, sc BLO in each st and ch to last st, 1 sc.

CABLE PROJECT

Morning Mist Shawl

The Morning Mist shawl is worked from one side corner to the opposite side, with increases placed along the wingspan, making it easily adjustable by working fewer or more row pattern repeats.

The design alternates between three stitch patterns: single-crochet ribbing, eyelets, and gentle, narrow cables. The cables are made of two waves with one ridge in each and 11 stitches per arch, featuring a front-to-back twist.

Morning Mist brings a sense of calm and quiet, like those early mornings when everything is still, wrapped in a soft, mysterious mist. It has a peaceful, gentle feel that makes the shawl both relaxing to make and soothing to wear.

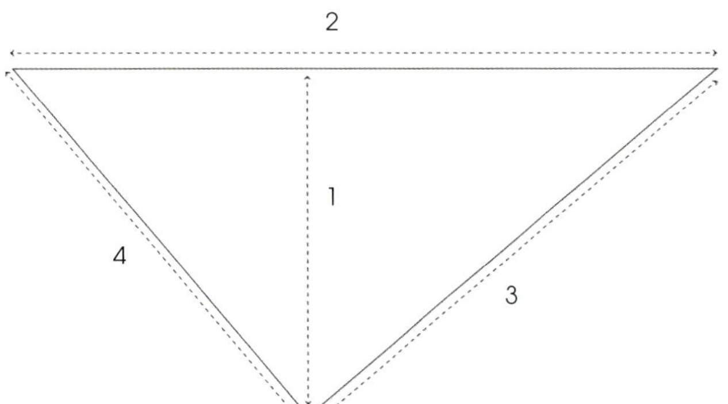

YOU WILL NEED

YARN

Malabrigo Arroyo (100% superwash Merino wool), DK/Sport; 100g (306m/335yds), in the following shade:

Peggy (AR334); 3 skeins

HOOKS

Size 4.5mm (US 7) hook

TENSION

19 sts and 20 rows measure 10 x 10cm (4 x 4in) over single-crochet ribbing pattern using a 4.5mm (US 7) hook

MEASUREMENTS

Depth (1): 65cm (25½in)

Wingspan (2): 147cm (58in)

Right side (3): 112cm (44in)

Left side (4): 96cm (37¾in)

ABBREVIATIONS

BLO	back loop only
ch	chain
ch-sp	chain space
PM	place marker
rep	repeat
RS	right side of work
sc	single crochet
sk	skip/miss
sp	space
st(s)	stitch(es)
WS	wrong side of work
yo	yarn over

SPECIAL STITCHES

Foundation single crochet (fsc) (see General Techniques: Basic Stitches)

Joining foundation single crochet (joining fsc) (see Chapter 5: Special Stitches)

Extended single crochet (esc) (see Chapter 1: Special Stitches and Chapter 4: Special Stitches)

INSTRUCTIONS

Note: *starting chains do not count as sts throughout.*

Row 1 (WS): Make a magic ring, ch 1, 2 sc in ring. Turn. (2 sts)

Row 2 (RS): Ch 1, 2 sc BLO in first st, 1 sc. Turn. (3 sts)

Row 3: Ch 1, 2 sc BLO, 2 sc in last st. Turn. (4 sts)

Row 4: Ch 1, 2 sc BLO in first st, 1 sc BLO in each st to last st, 1 sc. Turn. (5 sts)

Row 5: Ch 1, 1 sc BLO in each st to last st, 2 sc in last st. Turn. (1 st increased)

Row 6: Ch 1, 2 sc BLO in first st, 1 sc BLO in each st to last st, 1 sc. Turn. (1 st increased)

Rows 7–10: Rep Rows 5 and 6 twice more. (11 sts)

LACE

Row 11: Ch 1, 1 esc, ch 1, sk 1 st, *esc in back loops of 2 sts at the same time, ch 1; rep from * to last st, 2 esc in last st. Turn. (1 st increased)

Row 12: Ch 1, 2 sc in first st, 1 sc in each st and ch-sp to end. Turn. (1 st increased)

Rows 13 and 14: Rep Rows 11 and 12. (15 sts)

RIBBING

Rows 15 and 16: Rep Rows 5 and 6. (17 sts)

FIRST CABLE

Wave 1

Row 17: Ch 1, 5 sc BLO, 1 esc, 11 fsc, sk 7 sts, 1 joining fsc, 2 sc BLO, 2 sc in last st. Turn. (22 sts)

Row 18: Ch 1, 2 sc BLO in first st, 12 sc BLO, PM, 5 sc BLO, sk 1 st, 2 sc BLO, 1 sc. Turn. (22 sts)

Wave 2

Row 19: Ch 1, 1 sc BLO, 1 esc, 7 fsc, using a front twist, sk first st under arch, 1 joining fsc, 3 sc BLO, 1 esc, 7 fsc, working in last 2 sts of prev row work 1 joining fsc, 2 sc in last st. Turn. (24 sts)

Row 20: Ch 1, 2 sc BLO in first st, 6 sc BLO, PM, 5 sc BLO, sk 1 st, 10 sc BLO, 1 sc. Turn.

JOINING

Row 21: Ch 1, 6 sc BLO, *ch 1, starting in next marked st work 5 sc BLO; rep from * to last 3 sts, 2 sc BLO, 2 sc in last st. Turn. (20 sts, 2 ch-sp)

Row 22: Ch 1, sc BLO in each st and ch to last st, 1 sc. Turn. (23 sts)

LACE

Rows 23–26: Rep Rows 11 and 12 twice. (27 sts)

RIBBING

Rows 27 and 28: Rep Rows 5 and 6. (29 sts)

SECOND CABLE

Wave 1

Row 29: Ch 1, 5 sc BLO, 1 esc, 11 fsc, *sk 7 sts, 1 joining fsc, 3 sc BLO, 1 esc, 11 fsc; rep from * to last 13 sts, sk 7 sts, 1 joining fsc, 2 sc BLO, 2 sc in last st. Turn. (38 sts)

Row 30: Ch 1, 2 sc BLO in first st, 2 sc BLO, *10 sc BLO, PM, 5 sc BLO, sk 1 st; rep from * to last 3 sts, 2 sc BLO, 1 sc. Turn. (37 sts)

Wave 2

Row 31: Ch 1, 1 sc BLO, 1 esc, 7 fsc, *using a front twist, sk first st under arch, 1 joining fsc, 3 sc BLO, 1 esc, 11 fsc; rep from * to last arch, sk first st under arch, 1 joining fsc, 3 sc BLO, 1 esc, 7 fsc, working in last 2 sts of prev row work 1 joining fsc, 2 sc in last st. Turn. (40 sts)

Row 32: Ch 1, 2 sc BLO in first st, 6 sc BLO, PM, 5 sc BLO, *sk 1 st, 10 sc BLO, PM, 5 sc BLO; rep from * to last 12 sts, sk 1 st, 10 sc BLO, 1 sc. (39 sts)

JOINING

Row 33: Ch 1, 6 sc BLO, *ch 1, starting in next marked st work 5 sc BLO; rep from * to last 3 sts, 2 sc BLO, 2 sc in last st. Turn. (30 sts, 4 ch-sps)

Row 34: Ch 1, 1 sc BLO in each st and ch to last st, 1 sc. Turn. (35 sts)

LACE

Rows 35-38: Rep Rows 11 and 12 twice. (39 sts)

RIBBING

Rows 39 and 40: Rep Rows 5 and 6. (41 sts)

Rows 41-172: Rep Rows 29–40 another 11 times. (173 sts)

Fasten off.

FINISHING

Wet block your shawl to the finished measurements. Do not be afraid to stretch the fabric aggressively to help reveal the cables and lace. The difference in size and texture will be huge after blocking.

Starting from any corner lay the wet shawl out. Make sure the sections are the same width and form parallel lines, with the increase edge forming a smooth diagonal line. Working from the starting corner to the finished edge, shape and stretch the entire shawl. Pin it at the sides and allow it to dry completely.

General Techniques

BASIC STITCHES

CHAIN (CH)

Many crochet projects start by making a length of chain.

Begin with a slip knot on the hook. Hold the hook in your dominant hand and the base of the slip knot with the left thumb and forefinger of the other hand. Take the working yarn over the hook – abbreviated as yo (A) – twist the hook counterclockwise to catch the yarn and pull it through the slip knot (B) to create a new chain stitch (C). Continue until you have the required number of chain stitches, gently pulling down on the chain as you go.

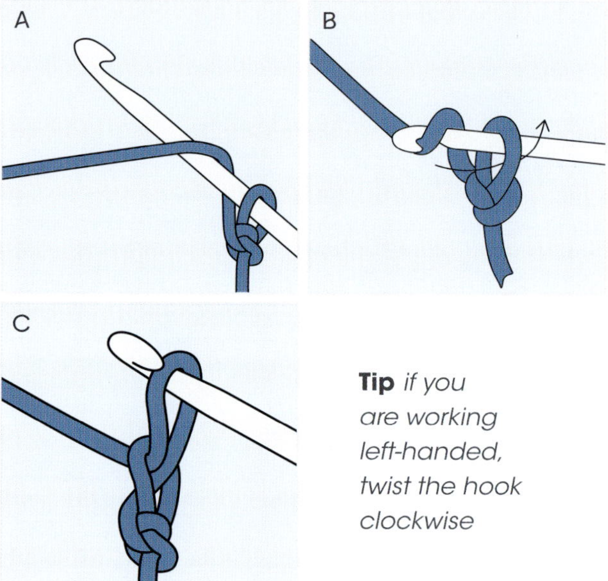

Tip *if you are working left-handed, twist the hook clockwise*

MAGIC RING

Wrap the yarn a couple of times around your two middle fingers and hold it securely with your thumb (D). Insert the hook into the loop and catch the ball-end of the yarn (E), pull it through and make a chain stitch to secure (F). Make the first round of stitches into the loop, then pull the yarn tail to tighten the loop. Slip stitch in the first stitch to join.

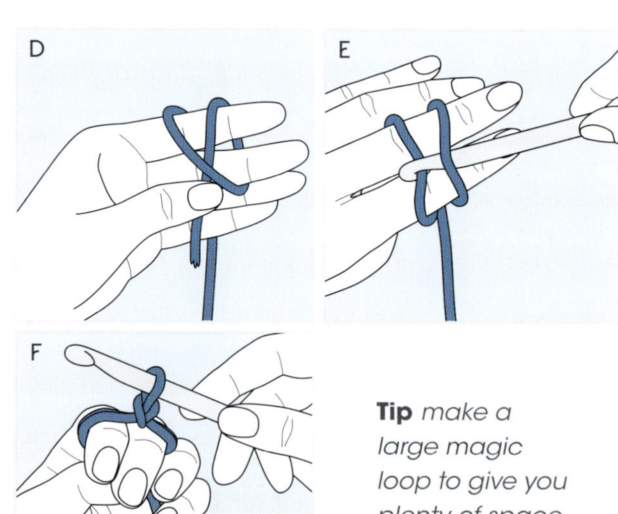

Tip *make a large magic loop to give you plenty of space to work into*

WORKING INTO THE BACK RIDGE (BUMP) OF THE STARTING CHAIN

After you have made your starting chain, you will see that on the back of each link of the chain there is a small bump. When working the first row, insert the hook into the bump (G) to create a neat edge.

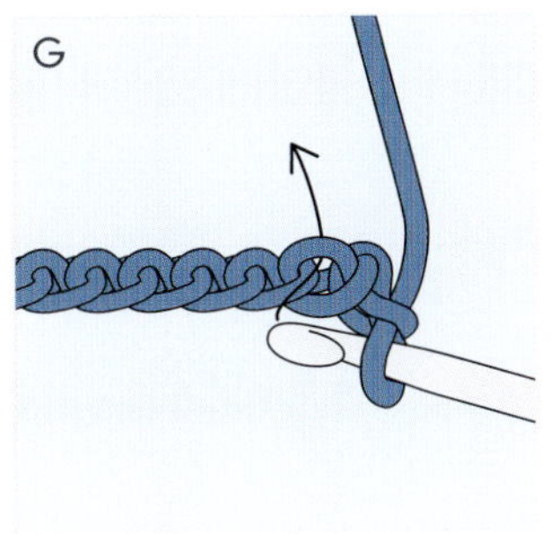

Tip *you can work into any loop of the stitch, but this creates a neat edge*

SINGLE CROCHET (SC)

Insert the hook into the stitch from front to back, yarn over hook and pull through the st (H). You now have two loops on the hook. Yarn over again and pull through both loops on hook (I) to complete the stitch (J).

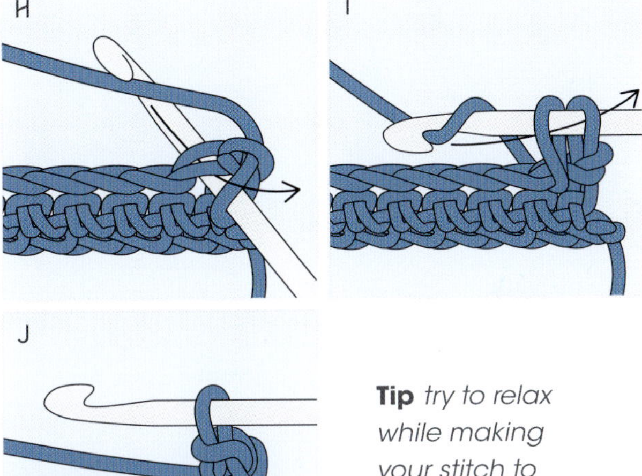

Tip *try to relax while making your stitch to ensure an even tension (gauge)*

SINGLE CROCHET 2 STITCHES TOGETHER (SC2TOG)

Insert the hook in the first stitch, yarn over and pull a loop through the stitch (two loops on hook). Insert the hook in the second stitch (K), yarn over and pull a loop through the stitch (three loops on hook). Yarn over and pull through all three loops to complete the stitch (L).

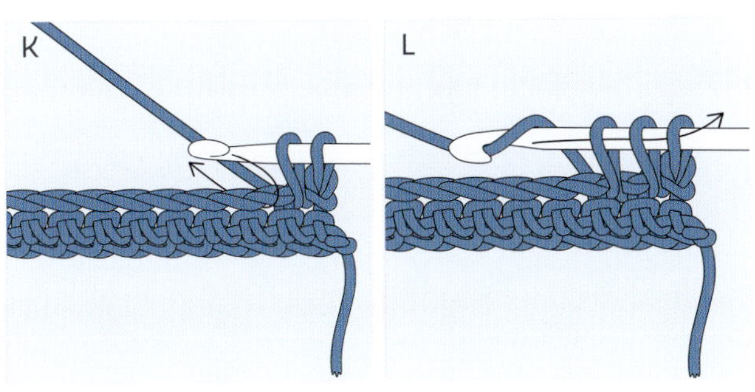

BACK LOOP OR FRONT LOOP ONLY (BLO/FLO)

Each stitch has two loops on the top edge. To work into the back loop, insert the hook in to the loop furthest from you from front to back (M). To work into the front loop, insert the hook into the loop closest to you from front to back (N).

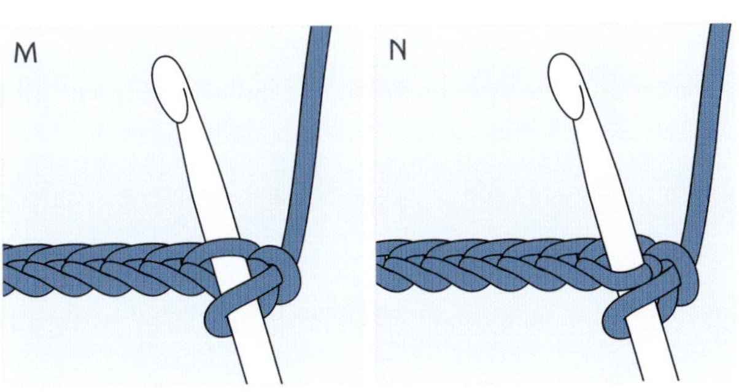

HALF DOUBLE CROCHET (HDC)

Yarn over and insert the hook into the stitch (A), yarn over again and pull through (three loops on hook) (B). Yarn over and pull through all three loops to complete the stitch (C).

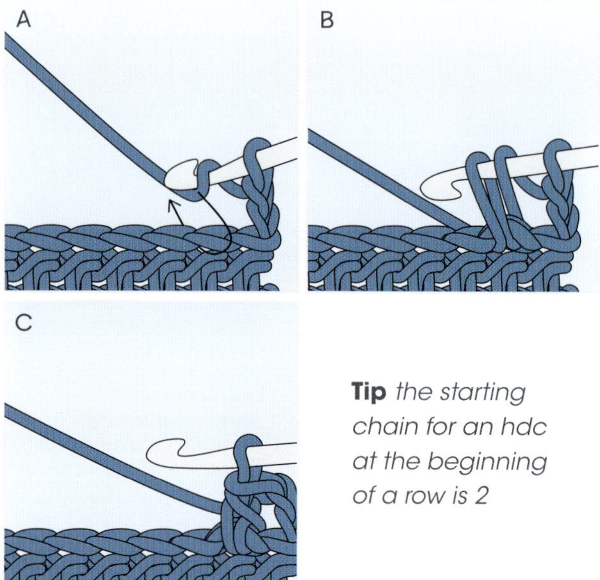

Tip *the starting chain for an hdc at the beginning of a row is 2*

DOUBLE CROCHET (DC)

Yarn over and insert the hook into the stitch, yarn over again and pull through (three loops on hook) (D). Yarn over and pull through the first two loops (two loops on hook) (E), yarn over and pull through the remaining two loops to finish the stitch (F).

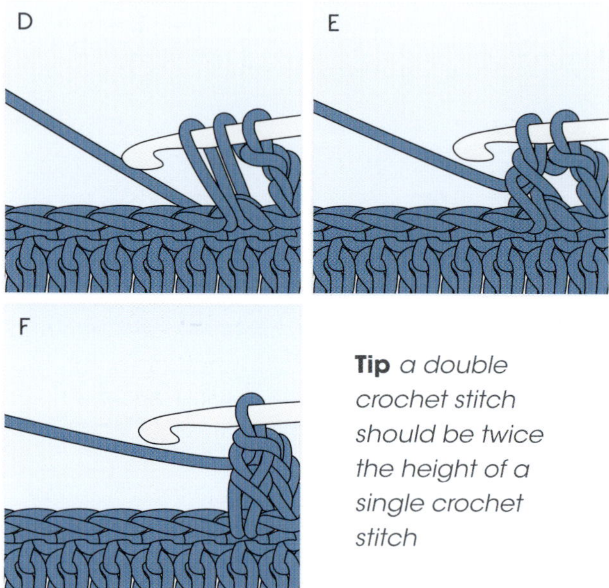

Tip *a double crochet stitch should be twice the height of a single crochet stitch*

HALF TREBLE CROCHET (HTR)

Yarn over hook twice, insert hook into next stitch (G), yarn over and draw up a loop (four loops on hook), yarn over and draw through two loops (H), yarn over and draw through the remaining three loops (I).

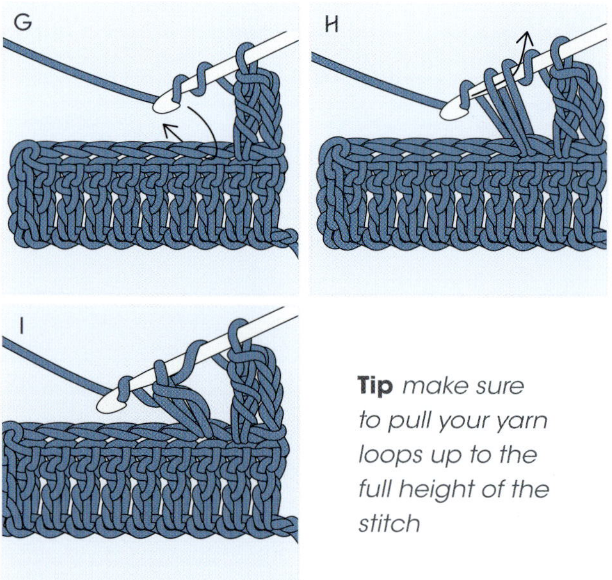

Tip *make sure to pull your yarn loops up to the full height of the stitch*

TREBLE CROCHET (TR)

Work steps G and H of htr (three loops on hook). Yarn over and draw through two loops (J), yarn over and draw through last two loops to complete the stitch (K).

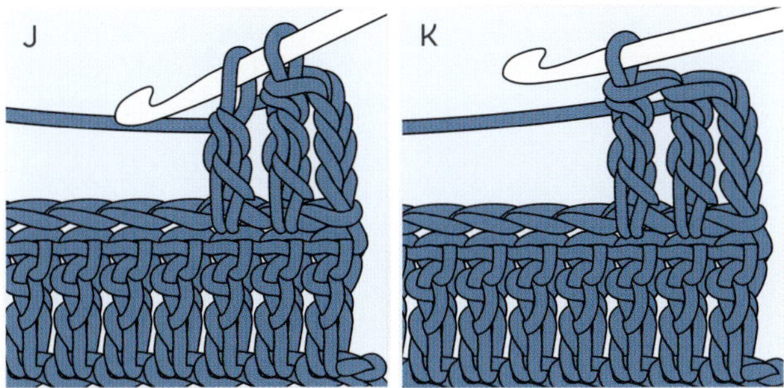

FOUNDATION SINGLE CROCHET (FSC)

In this book, fsc are worked into either an esc or another fsc. For instructions on working an fsc into an esc, see Chapter 5: Special Stitches. To work an fsc into another fsc, insert the hook into the space between the base of the last fsc and the stitch itself (L). Yarn over and pull a loop through the stitch (two loops on your hook) (M). Yarn over and pull through the first loop (N). This is the base chain of your single crochet stitch. Yarn over and pull through both loops to finish the single crochet stitch (O).

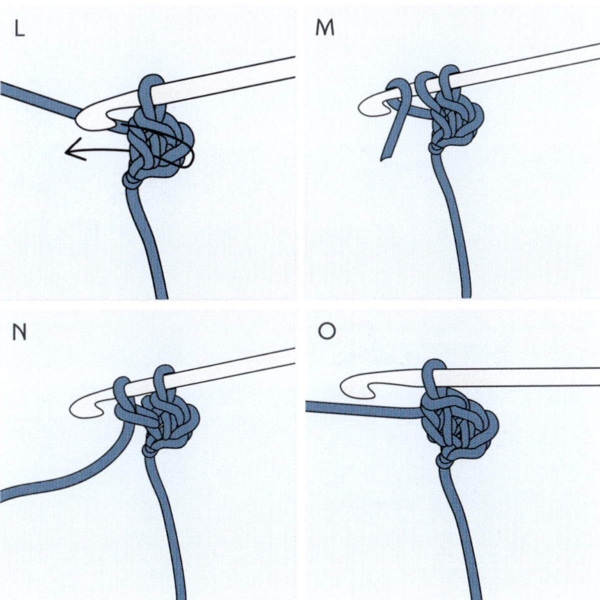

ABBREVIATIONS

US (UK) TERM	US (UK) DESCRIPTION
2tog	work 2 stitches together (1-stitch decrease)
BLO	work stitch through the back loop only
CC	contrast color
ch	chain
ch-sp	chain space
dc (tr)	double crochet (treble crochet)
esc (edc)	extended single crochet (extended double crochet)
FLO	work stitch through the front loop only
hdc (htr)	half double crochet (half treble crochet)
htr (hdtr)	half treble crochet (half double treble crochet)
Lst/Beg lst	leaf stitch/beginning leaf stitch
MC	main color
PM	place marker in indicated stitch
RS	right side of work
rdc (rtr)	raised double crochet (raised treble crochet)
rep	repeat
sc (dc)	single crochet (double crochet)
sk	skip/miss
sp	space
st(s)	stitch(es)
tr (dtr)	treble crochet (double treble crochet)
WS	wrong side of work
X-sc (X-dc)	twisted single crochet (twisted double crochet)
yo	yarn over hook

SPECIAL STITCHES

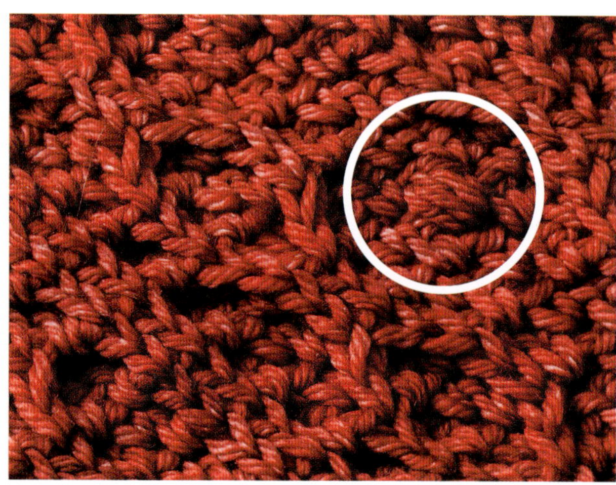

BOBBLE STITCH

*Yo, insert hook in ch-sp, yo, pull up a loop (3 loops); rep from * two more times (7 loops), yo, pull through all 7 loops on hook, yo, pull through 1 loop.

Note: *do not ch-1 before it as part of the bobble st will be counted as a ch-sp.*

BEGINNING LEAF STITCH (BEG LST)

Yo, insert hook in first st, yo, draw up a loop, insert hook in next st, yo, draw up a loop (4 loops on hook), yo, draw through 3 loops on hook (2 loops on hook), yo, draw through 2 loops on hook.

LEAF STITCH (LST)

Yo, insert hook in st, yo, pull up a loop (3 loops on hook), insert hook in ch-sp, yo, pull up a loop (4 loops on hook), insert hook in next st, yo, pull up a loop (5 loops on hook), yo, draw through 4 loops on hook, yo, draw through 2 loops on hook. On WS rows, work into the sts and ch-sps from back to front.

RIB STITCH (RIB ST)

Insert hook into second leg of sc or rib st just made, insert hook in BLO of next st, yo, pull up a loop (3 loops on hook), yo, draw through all 3 loops on hook (see Chapter 1: V-Ridge Stitch).

3-SPIKE STAR STITCH

Yo, insert hook in BLO of last st worked from back to front, yo, pull up a loop (3 loops on hook), (insert hook in BLO of next st from back to front, yo, pull up a loop) twice (5 loops on hook), yo, draw through all 5 loops on hook, yo, draw through 1 loop.

4-SPIKE STAR STITCH

Yo, insert hook in BLO of previous (just used) st in direction from back to front, yo, pull up a loop, (insert hook from back to front in BLO of next st, yo, pull up a loop) 3 times (6 loops on hook), yo, draw through all 6 loops on hook, yo, draw through 1 loop.

About the author

When I was a child, a world map hung above my bed, and every night I would gaze at it, imagining the far-off lands already discovered and wondering if there was anything left for me to find. Many years later, I'm thrilled to have found a vocation that lets me feel like an explorer every single day.

I've been knitting since childhood and taught myself to crochet at 19. It was love at first stitch, and since then I've only picked up my knitting needles for the occasional pair of winter socks.

If someone had told me back then that my favorite hobby would one day become my profession, I would have thought it impossible. The concept of being a professional designer simply didn't exist in my world. Breaking out of that mindset and discovering the vast, exciting realm of crochet design was the most challenging – and rewarding – step in my journey.

Today, as a crochet designer, I am deeply grateful for the opportunity to create, explore, and share my passion with others, constantly uncovering new possibilities in this craft I love.

Acknowledgments

I extend my heartfelt gratitude to everyone who has supported me along the way. To my family, friends, and my hairy yet lovable feline companions who, despite their best efforts to turn every project into a tangled mess, never fail to fill my days with love and laughter. Thank you for being my anchors, supporters, and constant sources of inspiration.

To the crochet community, your enthusiasm and creativity continue to inspire me daily. Special thanks to Malabrigo for providing the beautiful yarns that made these designs possible.

Finally, to all the readers and fellow crocheters - thank you for joining me on this creative journey. I hope this book sparks as much joy and inspiration in you as it has in me.

Suppliers

This book features yarns from Malabrigo, which is known for its high-quality hand-dyed yarns. Their rich color palettes and luxurious textures have played a vital role in bringing the stitch patterns in this book to life.

I've been using Malabrigo yarns for years, and they hold a special place in my heart, not only for their quality but also for the encouragement they offered early in my career. Malabrigo was the first company to provide me with yarn support back when I was an unknown designer with just a couple of patterns in my portfolio.

Their unique color palette inspires me to think and feel more like an artist than a crocheter, unlocking creativity and endless possibilities in my designs.

For Malabridgo stockists, visit https://malabrigoyarn.com/locate-a-store

All the tools listed are widely available online and in craft stores worldwide.

Index

A DAVID AND CHARLES BOOK

David and Charles is an imprint of David and Charles, Ltd, Suite A, Tourism House, Pynes Hill, Exeter, EX2 5WS

First published in the UK and USA in 2025

A catalogue record for this book is available from the British Library.

ISBN-13: 9781446315170 paperback
ISBN-13: 9781446315187 EPUB

This book has been printed on paper from approved suppliers and made from pulp from sustainable sources.

Printed in the UK through Buxton Press Ltd for:
David and Charles, Ltd, Suite A, Tourism House, Pynes Hill, Exeter, EX2 5WS

10 9 8 7 6 5 4 3 2

Publishing Director: Ame Verso
Senior Commissioning Editor: Sarah Callard
Publishing Manager: Jeni Chown
Editor: Victoria Allen
Project Editor: Rachael Prest
Lead Designer and Art Direction: Sam Staddon
Designer: Jo Webb
Pre-press Designer: Susan Reansbury
Illustrations: Matilda Smith and Kuo Kang Cheng
Photography: Tom Hargreaves
Production Manager: Beverley Richardson

David and Charles publishes high-quality books on a wide range of subjects. For more information visit www.davidandcharles.com.

Share your makes with us on social media using #dandcbooks and follow us on Facebook and Instagram by searching for @dandcbooks.

Layout of the digital edition of this book may vary depending on reader hardware and display settings.